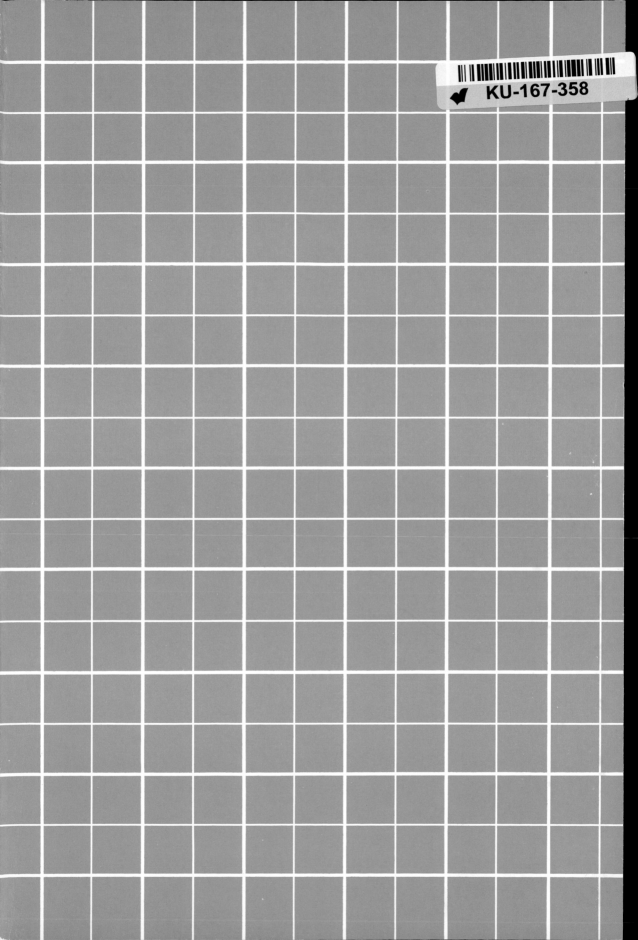

CONRAN
and the
habitat
story

CON
hab

Weidenfeld and Nicolson   London

RAN

and the

itat

story

BY BARTY PHILLIPS

ILLUSTRATIONS

The first four illustrations, showing Terence Conran and
an exhibition of his work in 1952: the two illustrations
of Terence Conran's home on Regents Park Terrace; the
illustration of his home in Dalham, Suffolk; are photographs
by Michael Wickham and reproduced with his kind permission.

Boilerhouse Project illustrations by kind permission
of the Conran Foundation.

Remaining illustrations by kind permission
of Habitat/Mothercare and Sir Terence Conran.

Published in Great Britain by
George Weidenfeld & Nicolson Limited
91 Clapham High Street
London SW4 7TA

ISBN 0 297 784307

Printed in Great Britain by
Butler & Tanner Ltd, Frome and London

Contents

Acknowledgments

My thanks are due to Terence Conran for giving me his support and the freedom to come and go as I pleased, to pore over the press cuttings and interview the staff and for letting me attend some important meetings; to the many members of staff at Habitat Mothercare and Conran Associates who gave me their time and their patience, both at home and abroad; to the many people involved in the early days who remembered them so vividly for me; and to Stephen Bayley of the Boilerhouse Project.

I would also like to acknowledge my debt to George Seddon for his objective advice and help in ironing out some of the confusion in the earlier sections, particularly where everybody's memories did not always coincide, and for his constant advice and support.

Chronology

		1951 Festival of Britain
	1952 **Workshop,** *Bethnal Green*	
Fabric design		
Designing and making furniture	1953	
	Showroom, *Piccadilly Arcade* **Workshop,** *Notting Hill Gate*	
		1954 Soup Kitchens
	1954 **Workshop,** *Donne Place, Chelsea*	
Designing and making furniture		1956 Orrery Restaurant
Designing shops and exhibitions	1956 **Showroom,** *Cadogan Lane* **Conran Design Group**	
Importing basketware	**Conran Fabrics** **Workshop,** *Fulham*	
	1959 **Conran Contracts,**	
Furniture design and	**Workshop,** *Camberwell and Fulham*	
manufacture	**Showroom,** *Hanway Place,* *Central London*	
Design group		
Showroom	1962	
Fabrics	**Furniture Factory,** *Thetford (Norfolk)*	
	1964 **First Habitat Shop,** *Fulham*	
	1966	
Furniture design and	**Habitat,** *Tottenham Court Road*	
manufacture	First Catalogue	
Design group		
Showroom	1967	
Fabrics	**Habitat,** *Manchester* **Habitat,** *Kingston*	
	1968 **Habitat,** *Bromley* **Merger with Ryman**	

1969
Mail Order
Lupton Morton, *Wallingford*
Habitat, *Brighton*

1970
End of Merger with Ryman
Habitat, Six stores
Wallingford Site
Mail Order

1971
Neal Street offices,
Covent Garden

1971
Conran Associates
Habitat, *Bristol*

1971
Neal Street Restaurant

1972
Habitat, Six new stores
Number of shops doubles

1973
Habitat in France

1973
Habitat, Five new stores

1973
The Conran Shop
Contract Showroom,
Avonmore Trading Estate

1974
Habitat, Continues to expand
Wallingford Warehouse

1977
Conran's in USA

1976
Design group
Barton Court

1980
Habitat, Forty-seven stores
UK USA France Belgium

1981
Habitat Public Company
Merger with Mothercare

1981
Boilerhouse Project

1982
Habitat in Japan

1983
Heal's acquired
NOW
Richard Shops
acquired

1983
Butler's Wharf project
Conran Octopus publishing

1984
Twentieth Anniversary of Habitat
New headquarters at Heal's building

Introduction

A small furniture shop called Habitat was set up in 1964 to sell the best modern designs in Europe which were not otherwise available in Britain. The idea went further than furniture. Habitat was a complete home concept, selling not just modern tables and chairs, but also a wealth of well-designed cookware and home accessories – a bizarre notion in those days.

Terence Conran, Habitat's founder, had come to art college in London in 1947 at the age of seventeen with no money, no training, a few contacts, a design ability, an 'eye' for what looked right and a knack for making friends and influencing people. When he left college, he set up small workshops where he built modern furniture, then he founded a design company, a textile company, a manufacturing company, a small business importing basketware and a contract furnishing company; he also opened a chain of restaurants. Conran was an energetic young man.

Yet for years he was eking out a living, financing one company with another. He became increasingly disillusioned with the retailers. Most stores refused to buy his furniture and those that did failed to display or sell it, or indeed do their job with any sort of confidence, imagination or verve. In fulfilment of a wish he had had for some time to sell what he considered well-designed furniture and show how it could be done, he started yet another company and opened his own shop in Fulham Road, London. Customers fell upon Habitat as though they had been starved of good design, which indeed they had. Today, few people in the Western world have not been influenced, wittingly or unwittingly, by Habitat.

Seeing the success of the first shop and realizing that nobody else seemed interested in following it up with anything remotely similar, he decided to turn it into a small chain and from that moment, in spite of setbacks, his success was written in the cards. He expanded his chain and moved into France, America and Japan; Habitat became a public company and merged with the larger chain of Mothercare shops. In less than twenty years Terence Conran had become a millionaire and Habitat a household word.

Like all successful ventures, there was an element of luck in Conran's rise. His vision coincided with the vision of his own post-war generation.

1

He offered what was new, modern, simple and forward-looking and gave the young a sense of self-respect. But it takes more than luck to achieve an enormous expansion and fortune within thirty years and to put it on such a solid footing. From a very early age he had the wits to grab opportunities as they came, the courage of his convictions, to see potential while it was still hidden and the ability to attract the help of the many people who admired him.

The secret of Habitat is the way Terence Conran harnesses his own and other people's talents, defines his goals, makes sure he has all the necessary factors in the right proportions, and sells his package to the public. His success is based on his refusal to be intimidated or thwarted, his prodigious optimism, an ability to deal with all aspects of business, his personal charm, an enormous appetite for work, and above all a clear vision of the way things ought to be done. He has always been convinced that, offered something better, customers will recognize and appreciate it.

Terence Conran has thus become chairman of one of the largest retail organizations in the world, and now that other stores can see the tangibility of his success, there is an eagerness to ape the Habitat style with bright, 'trendy' objects in fashionable colours. What other retailers fail to understand, even now, is that the Habitat package is based on a very precise definition and philosophy. It is not just pretty, practical or cheap. It offers a set of goods which looks as though it has been chosen by one pair of eyes and which has been designed specifically to fit in with Conran's own view of what is basic good taste. The whole Conran operation is carefully planned and efficiently marketed. The staff are trained to understand the Habitat philosophy and, with a share incentive scheme, encouraged to feel personally responsible for the continued success of the stores.

What Terence has done for retailing is quite unique and not yet fully understood by most of the retail trade. The obviously vital design element, Habitat's stock in trade, is only part of a balance of components of which the others are staff attitudes, training, marketing, display, promotion, advertising and price. The sound financial base he has achieved is the vital ingredient to ensure continued expansion and enterprise. Within this framework there is room for that flexibility and entrepreneurism which is the lifeblood of a shop whose customers have come to expect a constant freshness of products and ideas within a given standard of taste.

His unique view of merchandise and retailing is now being directed towards the baby business through the Mothercare stores, towards teenagers through the NOW shops, towards the more discerning, more affluent furniture buyer through the acquisition of the giant furniture shop, Heal's, and towards fashion-conscious women through the acquisition of a chain of rather depressing fashion stores called Richards Shops. This vast and diverse group manages to keep its particular view of style through its emphasis on design, the work of its own two design companies and above all through the flair and vision of its founder, Terence Conran.

In 1981 he gave an outdoor party for his fiftieth birthday in the grounds of his country home with champagne and fireworks, arrangements of vegetables in enormous baskets, mountains of good food, drink and music galore. It was 'better than the Queen's', said a guest. Mary Quant was there and so was Laura Ashley, equally people of their time and his. But this was just a hiccup in the business of business. In 1983 he was knighted in recognition of what he had achieved for design and for retail in Britain, but the story does not end here. Like all good adventure stories, just when it all seems to be over, it starts off again. Within a year of being knighted, he had acquired Heal's and the Richard Shops chain and formed a new publishing company. Habitat merchandise is selling in Japan and Habitat shops may well open in Canada and Australia.

There are plans to develop a section of London's dockland with architect Fred Roche. If there is a moral to this tale, it is that business acumen is not the only talent needed to be a successful retailer, but that dedication and an eye for design are the extra ingredients that can turn a small enterprise into a multi-million pound company.

1 In the Beginning

TERENCE Orby Conran was born in 1931 in Esher, Surrey. He and his younger sister, Priscilla, were brought up in a cream and white house dating from the 1900s. His father had started the family firm, Conran & Co., successful importers of gum gopal, until the advent of synthetic resins and the end of trading during the Second World War.

Both children admired their mother. Priscilla says: 'What kind of people were we? Oh, no money at all which threw us back on ourselves for our entertainment. We both feel our mother could have been like either of us. She always encouraged us and had high hopes from a creative point of view. She went along with childish fantasies and let us play them out.' Terence's admiration and gratitude for her are great. 'She never used her talents, apart from bringing up children. She had a good eye, could write well and did *The Times* crossword in five minutes – a sad way to use her abilities. A lot of the things I tried to do in early life, I did for her approval. She was an appreciative and understanding audience and was, I think, terrifically proud of me being able to do things she would have liked to do herself.'

Of his early environment, he remembers that his parents' home contained 'quite nice' furniture, but it was when staying with his aunt in Devon that he was first impressed by the way things looked – her marvellous house, its garden and the surrounding landscape. During the war he was evacuated from London to the Hampshire countryside but he recalls only a 'dull, ill-proportioned farmhouse' in Liphook.

In 1942 Conran was sent to Bryanston School, a progressive boys' school in Dorset. He showed no particular academic ability but a definite flair for practical subjects: he had a gift for metalwork and technical drawing and spent long hours in the pottery studio. He was taught pottery by Don Potter who was an important influence on Conran. He was a creative craftsman and had been a pupil of sculptor Eric Gill. A fellow pupil of Conran's at preparatory school, and in the same form at Bryanston, was Alexander Plunkett-Green who remained a close friend. He later married Mary Quant. He says: 'Terence was less of a child than the rest of us and I was rather in awe of him; he was a surly lad with some very strong ideas. He still is if you don't know him.'

Expelled from Bryanston in his last term (something to do with a rowdy party and girls), a pale, skinny seventeen-year-old entered the Central School of Art and Design in September 1947. His main subject at this major London college was textile design. Conran remembers 'sensible Miss Batty' who brought in design personalities to teach her students. He was taught fabric design by Eduardo Paolozzi, the flamboyant and energetic sculptor and textile designer. Conran assisted on a major screen-printing project for Ascher, the textile company, based upon Matisse panels.

Conran's reputation at this time was spreading. He became almost a legend at Central School and was known in other London Colleges. Stories circulated that he was paid £1000 a year *not* to design and that companies bought up and then suppressed his work. It was not only his work but also something about Conran himself that generated such tales. Before his course was completed he was offered a good job with the Rayon Design Centre, showcase of the then blossoming rayon industry, housed in a splendid old building in Upper Grosvenor Street.

The Rayon Centre's director was Dennis Lennon, the architect, with Maxwell Fry and Jane Drew as job architects. It had a design studio and exhibition showroom and a small monthly magazine was produced there. Conran was impressed with his job: 'Design in the fifties was fantastic; no expense spared. There were about four of us in the studio producing designs for any rayon manufacturer who wanted them. If a client wanted flowers in a design we would order blooms, not from any old florist but from Constance Spry. We put on exhibitions – it was all lavishly done. The whole place seemed like the ultimate in luxury.' He also worked on the house magazine, *Rayon and Design* but this was discontinued as the rayon industry began to decline. About a year after Conran had arrived, the centre was severely restricted and soon closed.

Conran then worked for Dennis Lennon, and continued to do so after setting up a small workshop with Eduardo Paolozzi, so that he could also produce work for himself. With work for Lennon, the workshop in Bethnal Green, in London's East End, and a small ten-shilling weekly allowance from his parents, he managed to begin to establish himself as a designer. Few examples of his work from this period exist: 'I kept nothing really of what I had done, which in some ways I find rather sad now. I was always slightly disappointed in them when they were finished.' Some of his fabric designs can still be found and work he did for the Midwinter pottery.

His marriage at this time to an architect, Brenda Davison, was not to last long, 'but we kept each other going for a little while,' he says.

The early 1950s was a bleak period in Britain. Much was promised; there was to be a sparkling new world to replace the dreary past and devastation of the war years. There was much speculation about how that world would look and how life would be lived. Conran already had a clear idea of how he felt the world should look.

1951 was the year of the Festival of Britain. Here was an opportunity for the best and most innovative of British manufacturers and designers to display their ideas and show the world that Britain was leading the way into a new era. Dennis Lennon was a prominent contributor and, through his work for Lennon, Conran had several of his designs displayed. His interior for Lennon's Princess Flying Boat could be seen in the Transport Pavilion, and his fabric designs and furniture were displayed in the Home Garden Pavilion.

The massive project of the Festival of Britain is much denigrated now, but at the time it seemed to hold some promise of altering the post-war gloom – for many it offered inspiration and hope. Dan Johnston, then director of a textile business in the north of England, and later to join the Design Centre, says: 'I came out of the army in 1947 and when I returned to work in textiles in the same small town I couldn't escape having slightly wider horizons. I could see that an awful lot of Britain was living in the nineteenth century. It may sound grandiose, but it didn't seem so at the time, to find the Festival of Britain exciting. I saw it as a modernizing influence, an indication that we were going to do things better than ever before. It pointed us in the direction of Scandinavia and simplicity.'

After visiting the Festival, Dan Johnston was so inspired that he went home and fetched his wife and two young children and his parents as well. 'In those days, to bring the whole family to an event in London was a very much bigger thing than it is today, but I was so impressed.'

In the period immediately after the Festival, the promised 'brave new world' failed to materialize. Manufacturers did not grasp the new ideas with enthusiasm and there was little sign of change. For the young and enterprising it was a period of frustration and worry. Conran faced the gloom determined not to compromise his ideas and achieved a great deal though with no financial reward. This was to be a time of hard struggle. Conran was even delivering his own furniture – on the London underground.

they could cope with soup. They noticed that the one espresso bar in Knightsbridge always had queues outside it so they thought they should serve coffee as well, but good coffee. Conran rushed off to Milan in a borrowed Riley and returned with a secondhand espresso machine in the back. 'I could make minestrone, split pea, onion – almost any soup I wanted – vichyssoise, tomato – all from the same basic stock without any skilled help. We bought very good apple flan from Mr Trueman in Bethnal Green, had cheddar cheese and French bread and butter.' And, of course, espresso coffee.

Ivan commissioned a grand sign which was painted on glass announcing Soup Kitchen across the shop front. The restaurant provided Conran with a unique opportunity to put some of his ideas on interior design into practice. The Soup Kitchen had the first tongued and grooved wall coverings; table tops were tiled; the counter was slate; a vegetable engraving from the eighteenth century was used as a motif; the floor was quarry tiles and the stools cane-topped. Here was a prototype of the Conran style: bright, clean, uncluttered and relaxed, using natural materials where possible for their texture and man-made materials for their durability. The first Soup Kitchen was an early expression of his combined enthusiasms for the good things in life and the modern. It also showed his rare ability to transform ideas into a practical project.

'When it opened, in rushed all these tramps and sat down. They thought it was a charity soup kitchen.' Luckily a reporter, a 'rather bright girl', from the *Evening News* came in at the same time and made a good story out of it. As a result, the next night the whole cast from the Coliseum production of *Guys and Dolls* came in to find out what was going on – and that attracted many more. It became smart to be seen there, rather daring. Conran and Storey charged nine pence for a pint of soup served in blue-and-white-striped pottery.

Three more Soup Kitchens opened, one in Wilton Place in Belgravia, another in Shoe Lane, off Fleet Street, and another in Cambridge. The latter proved to be a disaster: 'There was so much space there, we put a hen run in the middle,' says Conran. Students stayed all evening, talking and arguing over one cup of coffee or a bowl of soup. Though the huge place looked constantly busy, it was not selling enough food to make money. The London Soup Kitchens were highly successful, however, and Conran continued to work on his furniture during the day.

In 1953 he moved the workshop again, this time to Notting Hill Gate, to a place under the home of the Ballet Rambert, a location nobody else wanted because of the 'terrible pounding noise of the dancers' feet. At last I was able to employ somebody. It was still the time of rationing and clothing coupons and terribly difficult to get raw materials such as metal or cotton. It really was so difficult. I remember having to find foremen on building sites to sell me bits of metal and going to markets in Bethnal Green to find a piece of cotton fabric I could print on.'

Hard going though everything was, he opened a showroom in 1953 in the basement of a flower shop in Piccadilly Arcade. 'The man who ran the shop used to take a lot of plant containers from me. The room measured only about twenty feet by thirty feet, but we got it for thirty bob a week. An amazing young man, a deb's delight called Brinsley Black, became sales manager. He was extremely good looking with an endless series of girlfriends who took him to Fortnum's Soda Bar; a charming man, our first sales manager.' The showroom was the beginning of commerce proper. 'It seemed to make up my mind that what I wanted was to make furniture.'

On sale were terracotta plant pots on metal stands and cane chairs on metal frames, and other modern designs. Things were beginning to look up. In 1954 the workshop moved to premises with three storeys of space, in Donne Place, Chelsea, then the centre of bohemian life in London. For Conran 'it was a real breakthrough'. To help him he now hired 'two chaps, one professional and one amateur – one of them was a sculptor from Australia who had come here to have his teeth done on the National Health and he could weld'.

They produced plant pots, stools, cane seats, chairs, tables and more, and they were selling now to coffee bars, restaurants and universities.

The Soup Kitchens in London continued to thrive but eventually, Conran recalls, 'Ivan got ambitious and wanted to do salads and hot meals and so forth. I felt it should remain absolutely simple, so in 1955 he bought my share for £2500. It was really what I wanted. Those Soup Kitchens have spawned a lot of other restaurants since – the Stockpots in London were started by a manager of ours.'

The end of one project saw the beginning of another – Conran started a new restaurant the next year. He found 'a nice Georgian house' in the King's Road which was cleanly converted and provided an excellent location. He opened in October 1956. 'I called it Orrery because I was fascinated by orreries – they plot the paths of planets in relation to the earth; I liked the object.' With a coffee bar and restaurant and big garden at the back, paved in slabs, it was 'the only open-air restaurant at that time'. Conran worked at the furniture business during the day and at The Orrery in the evenings and Sundays. 'I had a mad Polish chef who loved showing off, so I spent all my time slaving away in the kitchen.' His sister came up in her holidays to help out and an exhibition of her photographs was displayed inside. 'All the girls who served worked unpaid because they loved him so much,' a friend remembers.

It was at the restaurant that Conran met Shirley Pearce, whom he was to marry. She was with Lord Queensberry, at the time, trying to look into the restaurant 'when this whey-faced lad in red braces came out and said "Why not come and criticize it from inside?" '

The King's Road was beginning to show signs of what it was to become in the sixties: a street which epitomized the style and creativity that made England swing. In 1955 Mary Quant opened Bazaar there, with her husband, Alexander Plunkett-Green, and their friend Archie McNair. Bazaar was a women's fashion shop, displaying Quant's highly original designs, and they opened a restaurant beneath it. The shop was designed by a student architect friend of the Plunkett-Green's. 'We were all straight from art school and the architect hadn't finished his course,' Mary Quant says. 'We knew nothing at all; we didn't even realize you had to get planning permission. When the conversion was complete the planning office said, "You'll have to put that all back, you know". I went and sat in the London County Council offices and cried an awful lot and in the end we got away with it.'

The shop was small and simple but its impact was enormous. Quant clothes were regarded as highly bizarre at the time. 'The day we changed the shop window, there would be a crowd fifteen deep shouting with laughter or rage, shaking their umbrellas in paroxysms of anger. People used to come from all over London just to look. It was so unlike anything that had been seen before – sort of scandalous really. But ten per cent of the people bought from us, we even had to keep the door locked and let customers in one by one.' Bazaar was not run along conventional business lines. The shop would reopen in the evenings in order to catch people leaving the restaurant below. 'The shop inspectors came along one evening and wanted to know who our employers were, because we were being unfairly exploited.'

Conran was fascinated – Bazaar was a key influence in his slowly developing idea to venture into retailing himself. In 1957 he designed, and built, a new Bazaar shop. He put great bales of fabric high on the wall and a free staircase up the middle with the clothes underneath.

13

Mary Quant remembers: 'A couple of days before the opening he spent all night with a dustpan and brush. He was never too grand to do anything himself. That was when the international trade began to take us seriously. We had marvellous shows with the models coming down the airy staircase.'

Conran had married Shirley Pearce in 1956. A friend recalls: 'When Shirley first appeared on the scene we all thought she was delicious; there was a nice smell about her.' From this time until the early sixties, Terence and Shirley saw 'an awful lot' of the Plunkett-Greens. Mary Quant says, 'Terence had a gilded feeling of success about him before anybody else. There used to be page after page written about the Conrans in *House and Garden*, in their Regents Park Terrace house. Terence and Shirley never arrived anywhere except on the run. That was supposed to be good for their staff's morale. If we'd spent a long time over lunch at a restaurant together, they'd arrive back at their office with a squeal of brakes and rush in, all busy.'

It was a period of great activity and hard work. Conran now says that, 'In retrospect the company was rather a mess then because we were doing so many things: shops, exhibitions, furniture design and manufacture, a basket company, The Orrery, the showroom, fabric design'. As well as Bazaar, during this period Conran designed the 21 Shop for Woollands, and a furniture showroom and Man's Shop for their main store. He also designed the Chanterelle restaurant. A new area for Conran was basketware: 'We were importing basketware from Madeira with Wolf Mankowitz, the entrepreneur and writer, and Johnny Metcalf, the advertising executive.'

The company was called Basketweave; it had been started from the showroom in Piccadilly Arcade in 1953 and was moved to the showroom in Cadogan Lane in 1955. Conran then needed a salesman for the furniture and basketware. John Stephenson, who has since played a large and sometimes stormy part in Conran's life, heard there was a job going. 'I was desperately trying to get into advertising and approached someone I knew in the business, Johnny Metcalf. Johnny said, "I can't get you into advertising but I have an enterprise going with Terence Conran and Wolf Mankowitz, why not meet Terence." I duly paraded at the showroom they ran to find it bolted and barred, which was an unfavourable start. I rang petulantly the next day and met this character who had started a curious little business called Basketweave. The classic conical basket chair with the metal frame was one of their imports from Madeira.'

John Stephenson became the salesman and trailed around the country having small successes, 'a shop in Sunderland bought some and then a few others'. Then the basketware company collapsed. John Stephenson remembers: 'The Lord Roberts' Workshops for the Blind sprang to life and accused us of depriving the blind of jobs.' Import restrictions were imposed on basketware from Madeira and the project was abandoned. John Stephenson stayed – there was plenty of scope for other work.

By 1957, Conran was designing and making furniture and shop fittings, continuing to design shops and coffee bars, had opened a new showroom in Cadogan Lane, off Sloane Street, and had established two new companies: the Conran Design Group and Conran Fabrics. He had sold The Orrery and was putting all his energies into his furniture business. For a long time he had undertaken many commissions as a contractor but now he realized: 'Why do this for other people? Why not do it for ourselves?'

Designing exhibitions became an important part of the business and John Stephenson became involved in the exhibition and shopfitting division. Conran's small team did exhibitions for the Atomic Research Authority, the Design Centre, and medical exhibition stands for a major fair. John Stephenson recalls: 'Terence and I spent endless days and nights at Olympia getting very tired. The drugs company exhibiting used to send quantities of samples and we found they had useful drugs for keeping you awake such as purple hearts or Drinamyl. They helped keep us going for five days and nights.'

In addition to everything else, Conran found time to teach at the Royal College of Art in 1956. A school of interior design had been established there and Terence was taken on as a part-time tutor, reputedly on £16 a day for one day a week – good pay in those days. He was under Sir Hugh Casson who remembers: 'He was a good teacher, as long as people toed his line, but he did insist that people thought as he thought.' Anne Moorey, one of his students at the time, found him 'utterly practical and in touch with the outside. Normally art college was where your parents sent you while you were marking time between school and marriage. Suddenly you were confronted with the Conran thing which was utterly anti-elitism and very down to earth. He had an electric-blue Volkswagen with left-hand drive which he used to lend us. Terence could hardly walk along a road without catching sight of something interesting and making it bear some kind of fruit.'

15

Conran was constantly looking for inspiration and adapting ideas for his work. A friend from this period was Michael Wickham, a photographer for *House and Garden*. He met Conran in his workshop where he had been sent to take photographs for the magazine. 'I found him welding various bent steel bits of furniture with pods on the end. Very amusing. I took to him at once.' They began seeing each other fairly constantly and in 1954 shared a memorable holiday in France. 'Terence says it was the best holiday of his life, though I find that hard to believe because he sat in the back of the car reading Ellery Queen most of the time. We went with my wife and Patricia Lyttleton, Humphrey Lyttleton's wife. I had a four-litre Lagonda and we charged through France staying in hotels some of the time and some of the time we camped. We went to look at houses, gardens and so on, like one does, and Terence kept dragging us into ironmonger shops where everything was hanging up in great bunches. Terence would say, "*This* is the way to do it."' That method of display he so much admired was later to be adapted for Habitat.

Michael Wickham's eye and understanding for English style, his interest in music, the arts, philosophy, food, wine, gardening, socialism, and his anti-nuclear convictions, were all much admired by Conran. He himself was so very engrossed in work that he did not have much time for other interests. He says, 'Michael is a man of great civilization and sensitivity.'

In 1958 the furniture workshop was moved from Donne Place to North End Road in Fulham, a place belonging to a Mr Lavender, forage merchants. 'We took this derelict place incredibly cheaply – £7 a week or something like that.' About eight people worked on the furniture. 'The foreman, Eric O'Leary, was a practical man of great entrepreneurism and energy. His experience had been doing castings, including work for Henry Moore. He just liked making things. The team moved in and did a lot of rebuilding and renovation to make the place watertight. For the first time the space was available to do both metalwork and woodwork. I acquired two of the most important people in my life, George Garner and Harry Hobbs, one a metalworker and the other a woodworker. Now we put the design office at the front in North End Road and there was an alley down to the workshop at the back.'

Anne Moorey, who had been taught by Conran at the Royal College, joined him as a designer and recalls those days at Fulham: 'I was the first person to be brought in as a professional designer. My drawings appealed to Terence because he never actually drew very well himself. I was paid a very good salary for a girl straight from college then, £700 a year. I went to this wonderful slum, his first real factory which was in North End Road with a food market nearby where we used to go at lunchtime. In spite of the dereliction, Terence's office always had style. There might be a bowl of vegetables on his desk as though it was some work of art; there was Arabia china in blue or white and he always afforded good quality writing paper with an orange heading for the furniture business, an embossed one in white for the Conran Design Group. We had three people on the design side doing a proper professional job in this hole, it was really very impressive.'

Yet not lucrative. The factory was not working full time because the furniture was still not selling well enough. The designs were quite unlike anything the buyers or the public were familiar with. The pieces seemed stark and uncompromising with their thin metal legs and strange spare shapes. Anne Moorey remembers 'periods of up to three weeks when we had no work. Then Terence would give us an A4 pad and say, "Just do furniture designs." On a bad day he might come waddling in and say, "Let's go to the pictures."'

Conran borrowed money and collected what he could from his debtors in order to pay the wages. 'He hated Fridays only second to the way he hated Christmas Eve or New Year's Eve, or any holiday,' says one friend. 'The workers were always waiting at the gates.' At one stage his account- ant recommended going into liquidation because Conran owed consider- ably more money than the business was worth. He went on, not purely through optimism, but because of the awful prospect of giving up. This made him try harder to keep going.

In 1959 he took an important step and moved the design studio and the showroom into central London, taking three floors of a large building in Hanway Place near Oxford Street. He went further and acquired a second factory, in Cock Yard, Camberwell. 'An exceedingly well-named place,' he says sourly. This became the woodwork factory, enabling the North End Road premises to be used mainly for metalwork. In Hanway Place he was joined by Oliver Gregory, who had grown up in Leicester and had cabinet-making training. He had been away in Australia 'to escape my working-class background', and had come back to show his Australian wife a little of England.

Christina Smith was taken on to assist Conran. 'I went off for a holiday for a couple of weeks before starting the job. Terence rang me in Cornwall and asked me to start early. I was supposed to be his secretary/PA, but on my first day I was thrown into a windowless room in the factory in Cock Yard to type out invoices.'

Contract office furniture was doing rather better than other lines. There were important design contracts, including work for the new Cunard liner, *QE2*, and two office furniture ranges did well. Though small fry by comparison, Conran was offering serious competition to the major English contract company, Hille. It was still a bad time financially and the domestic furniture was not moving. Philip Pollock, who had started Aerofoam, made the upholstery. Conran would draw a design on a scrap of paper; they would make an instant prototype 'which either looked good or it didn't', and if it didn't, they would try again. The first Chesterfield made by Aerofoam was drawn on the back of an envelope and Habitat is still selling it with great success.

They also made-up special-order furniture for architects, designers, nightclubs and restaurants. Conran produced the metalwork and Philip Pollock the upholstery for the air terminal at Victoria railway station. Pollock remembers: 'Terence and I were up all night because it went wrong. All my work for him was piecemeal and difficult to find. When I was making upholstery for him, right through his manufacturing career, he often owed me £10,000 to £15,000. He was relying on people's goodwill and was having a terribly hard time not to go broke.'

Meanwhile, Conran Fabrics was becoming well-established. The original partners were Shirley and Terence Conran with Cyril Winer and his wife, who were merchant converters with a small weaving company and mill called Victoria Mills. Shirley ran the business with Jack Winterbotham on the production side at first, and then Ernest Hirsch in Dumfries. Shirley Conran's assistant was Jeremy Smith who had first been employed as a general handyman. He says, 'I joined by chance in 1958 when my mother read an article in *Everybody's* magazine saying Conran was the talent to watch. I was looking for temporary work and this sounded like a challenge. I had done a year's course on telecommunications engineering and Terence was transferring from the workshop to the factory in Camberwell. I was hired to wire up the machinery and I did everything else as well – digging, mixing concrete and so on. He required somebody who could do anything without complaining, and who was willing to work all hours.' When that came to an end, Jeremy left to sail round the world with some friends. Conran remembers him leaving: ' "I'm off," he said. "Byee," we said. "Come and see us in two years' time." A week later a bedraggled chap came into the factory. "God, that was quick," I said. Jeremy wondered if there was still a job.' They had got as far as Cherbourg when the yacht sank on the rocks.

He became a salesman in the furniture showroom. 'The first day I was sent to look after the stand at the Furniture Fair at Earls Court. I had no inkling of what I was supposed to do. I was given a trade pricelist and told to evaluate whether customers were in earnest or not. People approached me to ask "Where's the G-Plan stand?" or "Where's the loo?", and others wanted to buy the decorations on the stand which were not for sale. One in a hundred actually asked about the Conran furniture.' After a fortnight there, Conran approached him, asking, 'Have you a feel for textiles?' He remembers replying: 'Possibly.' He was made Shirley's assistant and sent off to attend evening classes on weaving at Central School of Art. Dinah Herbert, then Conran's secretary, and Shirley herself, joined him on the course.

Conran Fabrics did their own hand printing for two years or so in a cellar in Notting Hill Gate, using a ramshackle old machine to bake the print in. They had more solid hand printers when they moved to larger premises in north London. Later they used professional printers such as Bernard Wardles, and Bernard Ashley also printed for them before he went into retailing with his wife, Laura.

Shirley and Jeremy Smith would work together in the showroom, sitting on orange boxes at a trestle table. He organized the orders and invoices; took orders in the showroom, filled in the forms and then processed them himself – cutting, labelling, packaging and posting. Shirley dealt with clients, looked for contracts and did some designing. She was clever with colour and created two simple ranges for the company.

The turning point for Conran Fabrics came when she captured a big contract for the P&O liner, *Canberra* – it absolutely swamped the tiny organization. Their usual order run was for two rolls but with this contract they were ordering runs of 6000 metres at a time. Every part of the boat was covered in a different material, the captain's cabin, the captain's night cabin, the chief purser's room, and each required 400–600 metres. Sixty different fabrics were eventually used, measuring over ten miles.

They then acquired the contract for the interiors of a fleet of Viscount aeroplanes for BEA. Non-flammable, laminated, mouldable plastics had not yet been invented so each plane had to be lined with flame-retardant cloth. Then, in the early sixties, as further education was booming, they did work for various universities including two of the 'new' ones, Sussex and Warwick, and for Edinburgh and a number of Cambridge colleges. The company used some innovative designs such as the Firecracker collection – plain fabrics decorated with stitched tape.

By 1962 the Conrans' marriage was breaking up and relations inside the company were strained. In 1963 they divorced. Shirley married John Stephenson and Terence married Caroline Herbert, home editor of *Queen* and the sister of Dinah Herbert, Terence's former secretary. One member of staff remembers going to Terence and Caroline's wedding one week and Shirley and John's two weeks later. Shirley left the company to go into journalism; John Stephenson left because he 'thought it the gentlemanly thing to do', and he took a job with Ogle Design where he stayed for about a year. Jeremy Smith found himself working for Terence.

Generally the company was doing better, with contract furniture still doing best on the furniture side. A contract to make salesmen's desks for the prestigious office equipment company, Olivetti, helped a great deal. The order for about twenty desks a week stretched over many months and, most important, Olivetti paid on delivery. Yet two major problems still beset Conran: his factories were not adequate and the buildings in constant need of repair; and the furniture was not selling well through shops. He had the responsibility of a staff of about eighty by 1960 and was determined to expand the furniture business. During the early 1960s he took two major steps towards solving his problems.

He felt certain he could do far better with a proper factory in which to manufacture furniture. 'I sat down one day and thought it through. I had two awful old buildings which were cheap but I felt if I was going to run a factory I had to be serious about it. I had vaguely heard of the London County Council Expanded Towns Scheme, a chance to set up properly out of London. At the same time I discovered that Fulham and Camberwell Councils wanted to develop our old properties which housed the factories. I was the perfect target for what the LCC wanted to do and in 1960 we started to negotiate to move out of London.

'It was the most interesting thing I'd done in my life: new towns were being created; my two factories were being redeveloped and the LCC fell over backwards to help us move. We looked at sites in Huntingdon, Thetford and Haverhill. Thetford, in Norfolk, was properly out of London and we liked the town clerk enormously – he really seemed to understand our problems. The LCC said it would build a factory to our requirements and rent it to us. It all seemed wonderful: a clean, modern factory by a good architect with space, plenty of it – so exciting.'

The firm of Hille had moved at the same time to Haverhill. 'I remember looking at their factory and being consumed with jealousy. But now we had money from the sale of our property to buy real machinery, and we began to prepare the staff for the idea that we were moving. We were contemplating a two-year period for the move and said we understood some people would not want to come with us. To show them what was in store, we took a bus trip of staff and families and let them see the council houses – quality houses, much better than they'd been used to in London, and we let it all sink in. In 1961, when the design for the factory was finished, we had a model built so the staff could grasp what was happening. Six months later we organized another bus trip for staff and families. The town clerk did the presentation and we met others who had moved out of town before us.

'I remember we regretted arranging for the local newspaper to be there because it was the middle of winter and the paper ran two headlines: "Icy Winds Freeze Door Locks on Council Estate" and "Rats the Size of Dogs Run Riot Through Council Estate" – they were coypus really. About seventy per cent of the staff agreed to move to Norfolk. The remainder were given eighteen months to look elsewhere for jobs and the LCC register of people who wanted to move out of London was made available to us, so we could replace those who didn't want to come.'

The move took place in 1962 and John Stephenson returned to the company at the same time, to run the Design Group. Along with most of his staff, Conran looked for somewhere to live in Norfolk. He took a cottage at Dalham – on the Suffolk/Norfolk border. He still had to be based in London so spent extended weekends at Dalham and worked in London during the middle of the week.

Hanway Place then housed the design team and a good showroom. Here, Conran became the first British agent for Marimekko fabrics from Sweden and for Jack Lenor Larsen fabrics from America, as well as displaying Conran fabrics and furniture. Yet there were still problems, and the move to Thetford had caused as many as it had solved. After such a major upheaval, it was inevitable that things would take time to settle. The move had also proved extremely costly.

A regular income was needed and to try and meet this he created a revolutionary new domestic furniture line. Summa was the first 'knock-down' furniture – a real novelty at the time. Each item was delivered to shops in pieces, packed in slim containers and designed to be easily assembled on the shop floor. It was created to avoid using precious storage space in shop stock rooms and to provide the customer with a piece of furniture which could be put straight on to the roof rack and taken home immediately – without the usual delivery delays.

Some shops argued they could not sell furniture which they had not inspected so for them the pieces had to be delivered fully assembled. A stand had been taken at the Earls Court Furniture Fair to promote the range and some eighty retailers put in orders. Among those who took the furniture unassembled were Woollands – the forward-looking Knightsbridge store. Conran had designed interiors for their men's department and their 21 Shop – a fashion enterprise, very much of the time. Woolland's had go-ahead buyers who appreciated Conran's furniture and their sensitive and enthusiastic managing director, Martin Moss, was very encouraging to the Conran enterprise. Woollands became the main London selling point for Conran furniture and proved to be an important influence.

Their furniture department was small but the most adventurous and modern in London. They were trying to get away from the 'department store gloom'. David Bishop, the furniture buyer, saw that Conran contract office ranges could be sold as elegant domestic furniture – and he did so. He displayed it in windows and everything he displayed sold well. Conran would go in to Woollands and sniff around: he was intrigued that this tiny department was selling a disproportionately high amount of his furniture. He often stood with the sales force on Saturdays and joined in.

Conran was facing problems with his new factory but his other problem was even more frustrating. The furniture he could get into shops was not selling to the public – except at Woollands. Few shops who took the range bothered to display it at all or showed any enthusiasm. He was beginning to think seriously of opening a shop for himself – inspired by Woollands and frustrated by the shops who would not do what he wanted. One of his major aims was to change the attitude the retailers continued to hold, which was to attempt to be all things to all people. Conran wanted to provide a coherent style rather than a general collection of furniture.

The idea of opening a shop gave him the same feeling of excitement as the Soup Kitchens had. As ever, Conran was looking for a way to create something new, practical and effective – providing a service he believed would be popular. And doing it all within his own sense of style by setting the environment and carefully selecting what it should contain. He had many influences – from French ironmongers to Woollands – and now he wanted to do it his own way.

2 Habitat

CONRAN had been harbouring the idea of opening a shop for many years but it was not until 1963 that he seriously began to plan for it. The time he had spent with the staff at Woollands – David Bishop, Maurice Libby and Kate Currie – had helped him clarify his ideas about retailing. Maurice Libby remembers that he was quite open about his intentions: 'One day Terence said, whispering, that he had it in mind to open a shop of his own. He chatted us up. What did we think about it? We imagined he was intending to start something rather on the lines of what we were doing in our small furniture department. Something smart and exclusive. He became so insistent that we got rather involved and interested. We asked if he would employ us. "I can't do that," he said. "My name would be mud, but I'll let you know when things are jelling." Eventually Kate Currie asked him directly for a job and I followed. Terence pointed out that we were asking for jobs, he had not invited us. But he took us on.'

Woollands closed not long after this. It was sold for development by Debenhams and the furniture department was moved to Harvey Nichols next door. There it failed abysmally, mainly because the managing director, Martin Moss, who had given it spirit, had gone.

However impressed Conran had been by Woollands and its staff, he was not going to repeat their formula – merely aspects of it in conjunction with other schemes he had for his shop. He felt that since people buy furniture so infrequently, they had to be drawn into the shop without making major purchases. The answer was to keep the shop busy and to provide a wide range of goods for the home – basics, such as china and crockery, alongside unusual items not available elsewhere, like paper lanterns and solid French cooking equipment (widely available now). There were many things he wanted to sell alongside good modern furniture. They would be displayed as if it were a warehouse, so that the utility goods appeared accessible. The shop would be approachable and friendly, relaxed and inviting. And everything would be sold with enthusiasm.

There were things he liked and wanted to sell that were only available in Europe. He would put them in the shop. He wanted to ensure that customers could buy a mug or a sofa with equal confidence, because they had both been carefully selected for style, practicality and value. He was providing a shop for people like himself and his friends, and hoping to convert many more – confident that others would share his taste, and his frustration at not being able to find lots of good things for the home under one roof in London.

There were four original investors in the shop who became the directors: Terence and Caroline Conran, Philip Pollock, who ran Aerofoam, and Pagan Taylor, a model. Each of them sank £2000 in the venture. Conran searched for premises and was able to think about buying stock.

He found a location which impressed him and asked Oliver Gregory to look at with him. Gregory was also impressed: 'We converted it, as I remember, for £6000, and did a lot of the work ourselves.' The building had a good basement which could be used as part of the shop and this made it a much larger space at a reasonable rent.

When Maurice Libby first saw the site he did not share Conran's enthusiasm: 'I thought it was a disaster. Out of town, nowhere near Knightsbridge.' His doubts were reduced when shop fitting started, designed by Conran and Oliver Gregory. He then began to get tremendously excited. With its vast glass frontage and spacious interior the place seemed enormous after Woollands' small department.

He began to lose confidence again when: 'One day a couple of trucks arrived outside. I was horrified. Terence had been to France. "Wait 'til you see the cookware," he said. There was a mountain of it! I was a furniture person and not turned on by it to a huge degree. We looked at the volume and couldn't see how it was going to fit. Terence simply replied, "You should see the acres of glassware, pots and pans, piled high to the skies in the big French warehouse. Then you'd understand the excitement of shopping in warehouses." We tried to incorporate the stuff into our scheme – laying pots on their side with aesthetic care and artistically draping cloths over them. Terence was appalled: "No, no. You've got to stack it up." It was hard for him to convince us and even to this day most shops can't bring themselves to do it.'

David Phillips, glass and china buyer at Woollands who later joined Habitat, remembers that in Woollands if he took a customer to the stockroom they always bought something. 'It's compelling, that warehouse atmosphere. We'd been vaguely aware of it for some time and, at Habitat, Terence initially did away with the stockroom altogether: the shop was the stockroom.'

27

Maurice Libby and the new Habitat team packed the stock on the shelves. 'We had to. There was nowhere else for it to go. Terence had to explain to us what some of the things we were going to sell were for. We were very ignorant in those days and didn't even know what a Mouli grinder was. Terence would drag us, almost unwillingly, to his flat for meals and there we saw a lifestyle we'd never experienced.'

When it came to the furniture, the people who had learned their trade through Heal's, Liberty and then Woollands, brought to bear their experience and training. They knew how to display and sell furniture they believed in with confidence and enthusiasm. At Woollands they had been dealing with a wide range of goods in a confined area – now the space was all theirs.

They stocked the shop with simple, pale, pine furniture; some large Scandinavian pieces, comfortably upholstered, such as a teak Mogenson sofa; the Chesterfield, designed by Conran and made by Aerofoam; and a Magestretti chair from Italy. Other stock, in addition to the cookware, included solid butchers' blocks and chopping boards, sharpening steels, butchers' aprons and unusual items such as an attractive red saveloy tin. There was also carefully chosen china and crockery, cutlery and cooking utensils, glass and light fittings, rugs and tiles.

The walls of the shop were painted white and the floor was laid with brown quarry tiles – it was simple and stark to the point of eccentricity by the standards of the day. With its excellent stock, including the best modern designs from Europe as well as good-value essentials, a display system that gave it the feel of a warehouse and music-playing in the background, it was a complete departure from anything that could be found in Britain.

Habitat opened on 11 May 1964. The staff had Vidal Sassoon haircuts, Mary Quant outfits and butchers' aprons. Freshly cut flowers were everywhere and a sense of style pervaded every aspect of the place. It was an essential part of trendy London and the swinging sixties. Being chic was no longer the exclusive province of the rich and established. Mary Quant had turned the attention of fashion buyers from Paris to the King's Road. Small boutiques were having an impact quite disproportionate to their size or clientele. Biba was a tiny shop in Kensington run by Barbara Hulanicki and selling inexpensive clothes – lean and skimpy and utterly up-to-date. Like Habitat, the shop was a total concept, carefully designed to set the scene for the clothes and accessories sold inside.

Habitat did not need to be expensive or exclusive to attract those in the know – it was *the* place to shop and be seen – but it also attracted crowds of Saturday shoppers and passers-by. The original staff vividly remember those days: 'An enormous number of theatre people and all the Beatles shopped with us; two of them came to furnish their homes. They'd rush in and skulk behind screens so as not to be seen. George Harrison and John Lennon were in together one day when suddenly there was an amazing shrieking and a coachload of schoolgirls descended, St Trinian's style. We had to bundle the two boys up a ladder and take it away, leaving them hidden in rugs.' Many of the staff were too embarrassed to deal with celebrities but Kate Currie, the furniture manager, would stand by the door and greet them by name. 'Lady Baker bought two Chesterfields in turquoise blue; Stanley Kubrick bought a huge kitchen table and chopped the legs off to make a coffee table. Carol White and Julie Christie, the film actresses, and John Schlesinger the film director, were all terribly shy, and Margot Fonteyn would die if you said good morning to her and wanted to be known by her married name, Mrs Arias.

'The Duke of Kent got his foot stuck in a fish kettle in the basement and though Princess Margaret never actually shopped at Habitat, Lord Snowdon came in from time to time and would say, "Darling, I only want you to show me around." Anouk Aimée came in to borrow furniture; Kingsley Amis and Elizabeth Jane Howard "did their courting in the basement"; David Niven was found fighting to get in one day as the doors closed, and Vanessa Redgrave is said to have bought leather-covered chairs to send to friends for Christmas.' Mary Quant was one of their best customers. If she was having a special dinner party she would swoop in and buy an entire table setting: cloth, napkins, glasses, cutlery, china.

Malcolm Riddell, who later became head of Conran Advertising, says, 'I queued up outside the shop the day it opened. I always had been interested in design and architecture and was desperate to have the furniture I wanted and thought I was prodigiously clever to have actually *found* such a shop.' People were enraptured by Habitat – so stark and brash and breaking all the rules of conventional furniture shops. Gone was the chintz and linoleum, the rows of sofas and reproduction furniture – here was a bright emporium for the home.

Caroline Conran was the buyer for kitchenware, china and glass with Terence. Pagan Taylor was manager and Kate Currie was furniture manager – she had total recall of every single customer, what they bought, how much they spent, where they lived. Maurice Libby was furniture salesman. Zimmie Sasson is described as having been: 'the lady in the black bombazine who was meant to look after accounts and paperwork – terribly bad as a secretary'. She spoke French, which was an asset, and dreamed of being a buyer. As soon as Conran put her in the shop she blossomed.

Within six months the store was bursting at the seams and Conran took over three adjoining units. They were used to create a fabric, toy and accessory department called Etcetera. Peter Hope, who had once worked with Maurice Libby at Heal's, was brought in to run it. Within a year, Conran made him manager of the shop. Pagan Taylor had left and married Oliver Gregory. Maurice Libby was put in charge of display. He resisted the change at first, feeling that his status would be diminished. 'Where I had worked before, we had a jaded type of display staff with aggressive manners and display people were always looked down on. The only display I was interested in was laying out furniture so you could sell it better. I had a feeling for laying out landscapes of furniture.'

The staff of the first Habitat were extremely enthusiastic. Many of them worked by choice on Saturdays because it was so exciting. The shop was proving a great success and Conran considered opening another: 'The early idea was just to have one shop. It had never been the intention to have a chain, but there was a curious lack of reaction from other retailers in this country so I started thinking it can be a chain.'

In 1966, two years after the first shop opened, Habitat was launched in Tottenham Court Road. The store's opening theme was nautical, with shells and ropes around the place. Posters in local tube stations declared: 'Heel over to Habitat'. A small publication called *Peace News* picked up on this and their headline read: 'It's War between Habitat and Heal's'. *The Illustrated London News* said: 'Tottenham Court Road is an even more discouraging thoroughfare than Baker Street but it *has* got Habitat and there is always something new to be found there among familiar Conran stuff.' Another report praised Habitat merchandise: 'Shallow wooden platters in many sizes, not dear, very pretty and inexpensive Indian cotton bedspreads, lovely lamps and ravishing deckchair canvasses, as well as sensible aprons and cheap china.'

The third store opened in Manchester in September 1967, followed that November by one in Kingston. This Kingston store was a triumph.

One paper said: 'The site is a gem – and was a bargain.' It was multi-level with 13,000 square feet of space and the most visually arresting store of the group. A multi-storey car park rose above it and the ground floor was terraced. The entrance was a bright red door and inside the brick walls were painted white. On the floor were brown quarry tiles and almond sisal.

The next location chosen for a Habitat store was Bromley, another outer suburb of south London but with not such a large shopping centre as Kingston. It opened in 1968.

Further staff changes came in 1968 when Caroline Conran decided to concentrate on her journalism and her children. David Phillips, who had been at Woollands, replaced her as buyer – the first professional buyer they had had. After a short while he was made a director. He recalls an early experience which alarmed him greatly but showed just how much could be sold through Habitat. 'I ordered some stainless steel cutlery from a cheapskate firm in Hong Kong, about 100 dozen of each piece, which was a substantial order for only three shops. The crook who took the order down put 1200 dozen. Terence confronted me, stabbing his fingers around and demanding, "You've got to do something." We reckoned it was about ten years' supply, but we sold it all in six months or so. I'd been a cautious buyer until then. I realized we could actually sell more of certain things. I was lucky enough to be at Habitat, not quite, but almost, at the beginning because it was the most exciting and fun place you would ever hope to work.'

Conran's 'revolution', as the *Evening Standard* put it, had in four years developed into a small and highly popular chain. Journalists were beginning to sum up its impact. Lucia van de Post wrote in *The Sunday Times*: 'It seems difficult now to reflect what the furnishing scene was like before Terence Conran and later, Habitat, arrived. So much do they seem part of what's best in our current design world.' The *Evening Standard* had high praise: 'Habitat is good, of course, with all its nice price furniture and rolling pins and bread boards, pestles, mortars, wine racks, the routine impedimenta of happy, wholesale marriage. In comparison with Habitat's great homeliness and cheerfulness, Biba's in Kensington High Street is quite bad.' Another report was equally glowing: 'There are superior institutions, Habitat for example. It's a splendid shop, the selling front of the Conran revolution with its tough, simple pine, its bright bargee colours, its attractive rows of unassuming glassware.' The *Daily Mail*'s Vivien Hislop was particularly pleased with the fabrics: 'Suddenly knockout fabrics in punchy patterns are giving a new look to Britain's go-ahead homes. Adventurous home makers are covering chairs and couches with enormous extrovert prints. They are making sheets in the new look fabrics, suspending lengths of fabrics as unconventional room dividers and dropped ceilings. There is an alphabet the most short-sighted child couldn't miss in block letters fourteen inches high, red, yellow and navy. Bright and bold for nursery curtains.'

It seemed that Conran would do no wrong but he was about to embark on a venture which could have proved disastrous.

3 Merger with Ryman

By 1968 Conran was considering the possibility of merging with another company – one which would provide capital he needed to invest in the Habitat chain in order to continue to expand. With five shops, good publicity and plenty of customers, Habitat was well established but was at a difficult stage financially. Profits made were being sunk immediately into opening and stocking new stores – each costing in excess of £30,000. The company was not overspending but nonetheless running up enormous bills. Conran was moving money from one section of his business to another in order to keep everything going.

The Conran Design Group had now been in existence for over a decade and had become the most profitable part of his business. John Stephenson had returned to work for Conran from Ogle, in 1962, and his energies were almost entirely devoted to the design group. Under him it developed considerably, designing products, packaging, interiors and working for Habitat and the contract furniture business, with its factory at Thetford in Norfolk.

The move to Thetford in 1962 had been highly problematic. Conran says, 'I can't say it was all bad. But it was a disorienting time for most of the staff because I had not calculated how very different it was going to be for them. We lost a terrific amount of money and I was worried financially.' The cost of the move from London to Thetford had been seriously underestimated. Added to this, the drastic leap from the workshop method of manufacturing – relaxed, informal and with everyone helping out where necessary – to the factory process was extremely difficult for the staff. The family atmosphere had gone.

Michael Tyson joined the company to become production director (designate) on 1 February 1965 and discovered that at Thetford the furniture was being made 'all at a time, by hand'. He made drastic changes. The factory was small, 40,000 square feet, so he extended the factory and erected a new building at The Maltings nearby, where the warehouse was then situated. This provided the company with 200,000 square feet of factory space.

Seventy per cent of the output was office contract furniture and special purpose joinery for hospitals and universities. The remaining thirty per cent was domestic furniture and, of this, about half went to the Habitat shops and the rest to small shops around the country. At times the factory was producing furniture at a fast rate but there were also 'nervous periods' when new orders were not on the horizon.

Conran was, therefore, treading a difficult financial path by 1968. He was then approached by Reed International, the paper group who owned two wallpaper companies, Sanderson and WPM. Reed were interested in a merger with Conran. The two groups could combine their resources, Reed could provide capital and they could use Habitat's outlets to advantage. A thorough feasibility study, looking into the economics and potential of such a deal, was immediately undertaken by Habitat. It seemed favourable and Conran presented the report, 'a great tome', to Reed in the summer of 1968. It was greeted with enthusiasm and all looked set to go ahead.

Then Conran got a telephone call from Reed with the news that they had taken over the giant newspaper and magazine group, IPC. They had too much on their plate to cope with Habitat as well. After the excitement and hopeful expectations, this was a bitter disappointment and Conran's next move was made on the rebound.

Ryman, the office furniture company, had been buying large quantities of Conran contract furniture. The Ryman brothers, Desmond and Nicholas, had visited the Thetford factory and everyone had 'got along charmingly'. Conran and Desmond Ryman, a delightful man, got on well together, and at one time shared a holiday. When the Reed deal failed, Desmond Ryman suggested to Conran that he should consider making a similar merger with Ryman instead. Desmond Ryman's enthusiasm for the scheme was magnetic: Ryman was a developing public company; Ryman and Habitat were both chain stores; combining their resources they could both expand, opening new shops at the same rate.

Conran made a hasty decision. Here was a chance to expand Habitat. The deal was 'thrown together' in a matter of weeks and the merger took place in November 1968, on the strict understanding that Habitat shops would be expanded at the same rate as, and on an equal footing with, the Ryman shops. Conran and Desmond Ryman became joint managing directors.

Disaster struck almost immediately when a fire broke out at the Habitat warehouse on 28 December 1968. Conran was woken in the middle of the night by a telephone call to find 'all that lovely merchandise' ruined. The premises were destroyed and the lost stock - furniture, china, glass, pottery – brought the damage to £180,000.

In addition to this, things were not going well with Ryman from the early stages. The business combination of Conran and Desmond Ryman started off well enough. Nicholas Ryman had suffered a bad accident while water skiing on holiday and was absent from the company for some time. However, as Conran became more involved with Ryman's, rows started. It became clear that the business was far from efficient, though on the surface it had appeared to be highly organized. The system of management was not operating competently and Conran could not bear to be involved in a business which, behind the scenes, was in chaos.

Conran was unhappy with the Rymans' rather paternalistic treatment of staff. He was considering a share scheme for staff but the whole idea was an anathema to the Rymans. The situation was made worse when the Ryman side made suggestions as to what Habitat should stock, suggestions which did not coincide with Conran's own, very particular, view of what they should choose.

The most serious problem arose as it became clear that a huge opportunity was opening up in the field of office furnishing. Ryman's had acquired a chain of stationery shops, Bedser Brothers, and these were being converted into Ryman office shops. The energy, and money, was going into their side of the business but not a great deal was happening for 'poor little Habitat', and, for Conran, the conditions of the merger were not being realized.

One new store opened in Brighton in September 1969, and even that had a Ryman shop in it, but there any expansion of Habitat stopped. John Stephenson was no longer running the design group but had gone over to the Ryman side of the business. The design group was then headed by Rodney Fitch who had first joined as a young designer in 1962.

He recalls, 'It was a good, quite prestigious group of its time, with about fifteen people on the staff.' Much of their work was in designing Ryman shops. Oliver Gregory was head of the design unit within the group until he became design director of Ryman Conran shops in June 1970. He remembers that all the money inevitably went into the Ryman side: 'Ryman shop followed Ryman shop off the drawing board. It was an exciting time for the designers, but there was never a togetherness in the company. I don't believe Ryman and Habitat ever really understood each other. Ryman's may have been aware of what the Conran Design Group was doing for their shops, but they never understood Habitat.

Jim Riordan, one of the Ryman directors, once said to me that he thought it impossible for Habitat ever to make any money.'

The other sections of Conran's business – the fabric firm, the contract furniture showroom and the Thetford factory – were more or less running themselves. But there was one development on the manufacturing and mail order side in June 1969 when Conran flew down to Wallingford, in Berkshire, in a helicopter with Desmond Ryman. Here they bought the factory of a company called Lupton Morton. This furniture company had been put into financial difficulties by two fires in the factory. They had been doing well until then, making the new style of modern furniture with foam upholstery and in pale wood. They sold it in their showroom nearby and through a mail order catalogue issued once a year. Conran was able to incorporate some of the Lupton Morton furniture, and some of the pages of their catalogue, into his own catalogue that year. The first had appeared in 1966 and Conran was then preparing the second.

Habitat shops were stagnating and Conran was continually frustrated. He felt that Habitat was 'so amateur' compared to other retailers, in particular Sainsbury, Marks and Spencer and Mothercare. All the Habitat people found the situation very demoralizing, and Michael Tyson, who had been running Thetford for five years, left in 1969. The Rymans continued to criticize Habitat and make suggestions as to what they should be selling. The relations within the company deteriorated to such an extent that eventually Desmond Ryman suggested to Conran that he might like to buy Habitat out. Conran says, 'I thought at first he was not serious. Then I realized he was.'

It was the summer of 1970 and many colleagues at the company remember 'that awful day'. Oliver Gregory was told by one of the Ryman brothers that Conran had ruined the family firm. 'For some weeks Terence had been very low. We had known him as someone always so resilient and strong and sure of what he was doing but for weeks he was dogged by depression and lack of drive.'

Negotiations were long and hard and Conran had to find a way of raising finance for Habitat in order to buy it out. Eventually he found a solution and Oliver Gregory remembers Conran telling him that he could buy out Habitat. Would Oliver go too? ' "Sure," I said, "of course I will." And from that moment everything was frenetic in the true Conran tradition.'

Conran officially bought Habitat back from Ryman on 1 January

1971, six months after the demerger had been agreed, at a purchase price of £670,000. Well over half the finance came from equity capital, the major shareholders being Conran and Midland Montagu Industrial Finance. Conran resigned as joint chairman of the Ryman Conran Group but he retained seventeen per cent of the Ryman Conran equity. He took with him the six Habitat shops and the mail order business, leaving behind all the profit-making parts of his business: the design group, the fabric company, the Thetford factory and the contract showroom.

Many of the staff went with him: David Phillips and Peter Hope, on the Habitat side; Oliver Gregory, on the design side; Jeremy Smith, who had been running Conran Fabrics. Jeremy Smith says he would have preferred, in some ways, to have stayed on in charge of the fabric company, but he had begun to experience confrontations with the Rymans. Today he is the longest serving member of Conran's staff and chief buyer for textiles.

Rodney Fitch stayed with the design group and John Stephenson stayed with Ryman's, 'somewhat stupidly' he now says. After Conran left, Ryman's was soon taken over by Burton, the menswear group, for £8 million. A large slice of that was Conran's. It is rumoured that Burton's imagined they were getting Habitat too, since the two deals took place within a short space of time. The divorce from Ryman was a turning point for Habitat, and for Terence Conran. It made him a very rich man, so providing the finance to expand Habitat.

After the Burton takeover, the design group did not fit into the new scheme of things. Rodney Fitch, with four of his senior designers, obtained financial assistance and bought the design group from Burton in 1972. It became Fitch & Co., and was made a public company in 1982. The group remained in the Hanway Place offices and are still there today.

John Stephenson stayed on the Ryman side of the business for two years as Assistant Managing Director and then went over to the Burton menswear side as marketing director and served out his contract there. He returned to Conran for the second time at the beginning of 1976.

4 Bustin' Out All Over

THE structure of Conran's company was somewhat confused on leaving Ryman's. Reorganization and a new management structure was required immediately to put the business back on its feet. Who did he have? John Stephenson, under contract to Ryman, was not available. He had David Phillips on the buying side, Oliver Gregory on the design side, Jeremy Smith and Peter Hope. Michael Tyson, who had left as production director at Thetford during the Ryman merger, was tempted back to build up the management team.

Tyson became managing director of the new company, Habitat Design Holdings Ltd. 'I was reluctant at first,' he recalls. 'Habitat had had a chequered career; the accountancy was never really good enough.' He took a week off and spent it cloistered with Conran and the accountancy firm of Arthur Andersen, one of the 'big eight' international accountants, and together they worked out a strategy.

Michael Tyson says, 'I rejoined the company on the condition that they would not start manufacturing again. I was determined to make Habitat a viable retailing business. It is always a temptation to Terence, from time to time, to go back to manufacturing. He gets a gleam in his eye and thinks, "We could do this so much better ourselves."'

Tyson had a firm belief in modern management methods, took a deliberately jaundiced look at Habitat and decided where the main problems lay: conflict at top level, low morale throughout the company, and too few stores. 'We spent months building it up by its bootstraps. There was very little management – no accountancy or data processing.' Being an articulate man with strong views, he and Conran did not always see eye to eye, but Tyson was usually able to carry a point and argue it through. He took a long term view of projects and of aims.

Ian Peacock, who was a chartered accountant and had worked with the Arthur Andersen firm, was recruited soon after Michael Tyson. He says, 'I knew nothing of Habitat until the suggestion came that I should join the firm. Not many people did. It was a minuscule business. I'd been used to big businesses and, to be frank, I would never have dreamed of moving to something like this except that the challenge interested me. I felt there was a fair chance of it going somewhere.' He was intrigued, also, by the Executive Share Scheme, an incentive Conran was offering. Half a dozen or so of the top staff participated in the original scheme. 'A share of the action is not often available to employees and that part of the deal made it a worthwhile risk. It was one of the factors that made us all agree to join Terence in what was, after all, a small, doubtful, business with no track record and in a pretty chaotic condition. Much smaller than anything most of us were used to.'

Conran had not officially bought Habitat until January 1971, 'so for the first six months I was working on my own,' he says. The Wallingford warehouse and showroom he had bought from Lupton Morton in 1969 with Ryman who held on to the factory, was now to become the showroom for Habitat. He had six shops, the showroom and the mail order business. The turnover was £2 million. Ian Peacock's first objective on starting was to try to make sense of the accounts: 'We had no idea whether we were making a profit or a loss. For the first year, to the end of June 1971, spanning the months since the demerger, part of the accounting was still with Rymans and very confused, and part of it was the responsibility of the new Habitat organization. We had a real hotch potch of records for that period. I said, "It's no good doing a normal audit on this lot; the only thing to do is to make sure the closing balance sheet is right. Whatever the difference is, it's the profit."'

A postal strike in 1970 gave them three months to sort out the mail order business which had come with the other parts of the Lupton Morton business at Wallingford. An orderly accounting system was worked out. Buying and merchandizing, previously merged, were split into two separate functions with one department doing the negotiating and the purchase of goods, and the other working out quantities, ana-lysing past sales figures and so on. From mid-1970 to mid-1971 the profits were £145,000.

The company was still in a demoralized state and Conran and Tyson saw that the best way of instilling some confidence was to open a new store. Bristol was chosen and a site was found. The shop opened only three months later, in September 1971, with a big party to celebrate, ensuring plenty of publicity so that they could 'really get people believing in Habitat again'. In the same month, Conran took part in a display, with Heal's and Times Furnishing, at the Design Centre, at which visitors could order the furniture on the spot.

There was an interesting account of Terence Conran written by a journalist at this time: 'His dark hair tends to be windswept, his pants are baggy and his blue shirt, rather than being slim fit, gapes a bit at the buttons to reveal a hairy tummy. Let no one be deceived by the gentle, honest, bumbling Conran style. He is, after all, the man who brought modern taste to the masses in the form of a package deal, who saw the Habitat turnover increase by a staggering eighty per cent in each of his first two years of independence. And who's to say the sky's the limit so far as future development is concerned.'

In 1972 six stores opened in quick succession: Cheltenham (March), Guildford (May), Birmingham and Nottingham (November), and Watford and Croydon (December). As Conran says, 'There had to be more Habitats. Always, throughout my life, I've had the motivation to move and expand. It's because you want to do things better. The reason for expanding Habitat was that there was no way of seeing if or how it could develop unless there were more shops. To do this, we wanted to develop the catalogue, have a wider spread of customers, more turnover. Then it became self-motivating because the people inside the company were themselves eager to expand and become more efficient. It became a sort of treadmill. If you say, "Stop!", it loses its virility. It is one of the unsatisfactory things in the human make up that if you stop development in business it fossilizes and you lose the bright young people who will keep it going.

'I was always jealous of other people who were doing better than me – Hille and Knoll [both furniture companies] were a spur to us. When we became professional retailers we realized we were inadequate in all sorts of ways. David Phillips and others came in to the business who had already gained relevant retail experience outside. We started talking to people like Selim Zilkha, of Mothercare, with his incredibly efficient business. We realized that stock control, the staff team, delivery systems, were almost as important as the merchandise. We began to realize that no matter how much enthusiasm we put into the business, until we had proper systems to support it we were wasting too much energy and creativity.'

Among the talented people who joined at this time, 1973, were Chris Turner, now chief executive of Habitat UK, George Rogers, who came as director of purchasing, and Alex Wilson, who was made treasurer and company secretary.

In that year new stores opened in Leicester (May), Liverpool (July), London (King's Road) (September), Glasgow (November) and Bournemouth (December). Also in 1973, the first Habitat store opened in France, and in London The Conran Shop opened.

When the King's Road store opened, the staff from the original Fulham Road store moved there and the first Habitat shop was put to a new purpose. The Conran Shop was to provide a showcase of furniture and household items that were more immediate, one-off and more up-market than Habitat merchandise. It could act as a testing ground for stock which might later move into Habitat. None of the merchandise in the two shops would be the same, but some lines might be moved to Habitat and out of The Conran Shop if they showed potential and were not too expensive. In a way it was to continue what the first Habitat shop was doing in the early sixties: offering quality furniture and well-designed household goods with the unmistakable Conran imprint.

The first buyer for the new shop was Maggie Heaney. She had been with Habitat since the early days, starting as an inexperienced sales girl in the Tottenham Court Road store. She was 'tired of working in dull secretarial jobs' when she saw an advertisement in the *Daily Telegraph* for a job at Habitat. She applied because working at Habitat was the thing to do at the time. She remembers her interview: 'I saw a most delightful man called John Mawer, who was very high powered in spite of the fact that he had only one leg and half of one finger was missing. My only selling experience had been on a stall of holy pictures at a convent school bazaar. The salary offered by Habitat to office staff was so appalling that I couldn't accept the job. Terence wrote back: "In view of your amazing experience I can take you into sales."

'One had to work astoundingly hard for what seemed like very little reward, but we were all so dedicated. Habitat was still a small family business at the time and a super place to work. Terence used to put the fear of God into everyone, coming in with a handkerchief and dusting the shelves. We used to be warned that he was coming to make sure the place was spotless, but he would find dust.'

It was 1972 when Maggie Heaney was asked if she would be the buyer for the new Conran Shop. She accepted and worked in Neal Street with the design group for a year or more, researching the project before actually opening the shop.

'I've often felt embarrassed that I had no formal training,' she says. 'Terence has taught me everything I know and that was a marvellous training. I went to exhibitions abroad with him and he taught me not to just rush out and buy one thing, but to consider it as a part of the whole collection, to see things together. I think this is Terence's success, his selection and his eye. But you have to learn not to be intimidated by him. I bought a lot of handmade soaps from France once. It must have been a bad day for Terence because he said they looked like a lot of turds. In the end he liked them though, and insisted they be in all the shops in both Britain and Europe.

'I went to the Birmingham Furniture Fair with him, and to Paris, but most importantly to the international fair in Milan. He was quite cunning because he would send the buyers on as the advance party and, in the early days, we weren't sure what to aim for, so we had to go around every single, massive hall there. Then he would arrive days later and say, "What have you seen?" and then we'd have to do the whole lot again with him.'

Several buyers followed Maggie Heaney at The Conran Shop until 1978 when Conran's sister Priscilla returned from living in France and took over control of both the buying for the shop and the display and look of the place. Under her influence, it became probably the most imaginative modern furniture store in London, with the courage to take superb furniture by British firms as well as foreign ones. It had an interesting lighting department, an exciting kitchen section and, in particular, an expanding textile department with many fabrics, some of which were specially designed and made in India. The shop has a flair and confidence most unusual in Britain. Priscilla's experience in Paris, where she ran her own antiques business, enabled her to include a small number of antiques and secondhand items, such as chests and cupboards, which added to the shop's personal style and quality.

In 1981 she joined the Habitat Mothercare Group Design but she has never lost interest in The Conran Shop and her influence is still strong. It remains the first port of call for anyone in the know who is obsessed with home making. It is staffed by a small team of genuinely devoted people who are enthusiastically convinced of the quality of their merchandise. In spring the shop is filled with hyacinths, and at one stage there was a marvellous smell of herbs coming from the basement. During a Guatemalan fabric exhibition, they filled the shop with a delicious coffee smell. The shop floor is replanned every six weeks by Stafford Cliff, creative director of Conran Associates (the design group), and Geoff Marshall, director and manager of The Conran Shop, Priscilla herself, the buyer and the display staff. The shop is arranged depending on the stock and the promotion at that time.

With the advent of the new Heal's shop, which is to be a quality store, it is the intention to retain The Conran Shop as a separate entity and to make it very stylish and more innovatory. Priscilla says, 'We aim to excite and please the customer. It is a very wonderful and exciting shop to work for, to the extent that I will inspect the windows in the middle of the night if I suddenly wake up and wonder if the display is right. I love the shop and believe it is a valuable part of the group as it grows larger.'

Another development for Conran in 1973 was his return to the contract furnishing field. The new company opened a showroom at the Avonmore Trading Estate near Olympia, with a warehouse alongside, both designed by Conran Associates. The doors were painted in the characteristic Conran deep blue with white tiles, red handrails, white walls and ceilings. The ceiling beams were faced with a pelmet so fabrics could be displayed there. There was sisal on the floor and the three-sided reception desk in the centre of the room was faced in dark-blue laminate with cream stripes. The lighting was on Lytespan track and there was air conditioning. They market contract furniture by the world's leading manufacturers. Early lines included David Rowland's stacking and linking chairs; the Kembo moulded polystyrene chair; the Kevi Series 2000 secretarial chair designed by Jorgen Rasmussen; the GF Body Chair; and Olivetti's new range of office furniture designed by Ettore Sotsass, instigator of the fashionable, avant garde Memphis Furniture group in Milan. Accessories were included which introduced an element of fun and human fallibility into the whole immaculate system.

Conran Contracts sold the GF stacking chair to St Paul's Cathedral through Dr Bernard Fielden, surveyor to the fabric and adviser to the Dean and Chapter. The stained, English-oak veneer seats, with solid steel frames finished in nickel, were described by *The Cabinetmaker* as designed for 'comfort, mobility and prayer'.

By June 1974, Habitat had an annual turnover of £11 million – an increase of £8 million in three years. During that calendar year Conran opened a larger showroom at Wallingford and further stores in Bolton, York and Romford (all in August) and in Coventry (November). In France stores opened in Bures Orsay (March), Orgeval (April) and Avenue Wagram (September). The *Birmingham Post* reported: 'Habitat is entering its second decade. There are nineteen shops including one in the Birmingham shopping centre and it is embarking on a massive expansion programme. New stores have been opened with the explosive regularity of corks at a champagne party.' By June there were twenty-two outlets in all.

When it left Ryman, the firm operated without any proper warehouse and goods were delivered direct from the suppliers to the customers. This proved to be horribly inefficient. Customers would find they waited weeks for delivery and mistakes were made – sofas arrived upholstered in the wrong colours. It made a very bad impression at the time. The new warehouse that was opened in 1974 was designed by architects Ahrends, Burton and Koralek. The site was at Wallingford, where Habitat had had a showroom on the old Lupton Morton site. Richard Burton, the architect, presented his plans to Conran at his office in Neal Street, Covent Garden. 'We were wandering along the street after the presentation and we still hadn't decided on the colour. I caught sight of a green Porsche and said, "How about that?" "Yes," said Terence. A week later, the complete back of the Porsche arrived in our office. It was his. He had driven into a bollard and sent the whole, damaged, wing as a colour sample. That's what started Habitat green.'

The building was painted asbestos sheet. Conran chose ABK as the architects because he said they were the only architects he interviewed who had spent money on their own offices. He had always had a keen eye for property and for a bargain and this building was extremely good value. Richard Burton remembers: 'Terence got an estimate from a package builder for his warehouse. He told us to scrutinize the package and see what they'd left out, things like lighting and so on. He was willing to spend twenty per cent more than their price in order to get a decent building he said. "That's your price." The building cost absolutely nothing – £6 a square foot.' He admires Conran's ability to make decisions. 'He was so clear about what he wanted. The building was publicized endlessly in the papers, it was a superb advertisement for Conran.' José Manser wrote in the *Financial Times*: 'Habitat's Handsome Shed at Wallingford. When Inigo Jones started to design St Paul's Covent Garden he promised his client the handsomest barn in Europe. A more recent architectural practice, Ahrens, Burton and Koralek have just given their client what must be the handsomest shed in Berkshire.'

At about the same time another warehouse was acquired at Wellingborough in Northants. It had been open for only about a year when Geoff Davy, who had started with Habitat in 1973, was put in charge of the operation. He was soon to become a key figure in Conran's team. Having grown up in the Midlands, Davy joined Boots in warehouse and distribution after university. He was promoted to management in Scotland but decided to move to Littlewoods and started over again, as a trainee. Littlewoods had an almost military discipline, 'full of young men with short hair and blue suits'. It had a sophisticated training scheme and Geoff Davy became a deputy manager in a medium-sized store. 'The only flaw was that one had to move around the country a great deal. By the time I left Littlewoods we were in search of our seventh home in three years. They provided company homes and would say, suddenly, "Next week we want you in Birmingham," and you would have to go. We found it increasingly difficult living with other people's furniture and apologizing for it. The prospect of a free house had been nice when I first joined, but I did not want to spend the rest of my life in houses of someone else's choice.'

He answered an advertisement for a store manager with Habitat. 'I must confess. I did not know who Habitat was. They were offering enough money to move and buy a house. I wasn't especially anxious to get the job – it was one of those ring-up-on-Sunday efforts.' He was accepted as manager for the Nottingham branch, doing a month first in the King's Road where he was appalled at the state of the business after the discipline of Littlewoods. He started in October 1973 and 'had just scraped through Christmas' when the three-day week started during the miners' strike. 'We had people walking up and down with sandwich boards saying "Habitat is doing it in the dark". The shop was lit by candles and paraffin lamps and they did their best to stay open, with a generator in the basement run off black-market petrol. I had to pay a fairground family in grubby pound notes for it one Friday dinner time.'

After the three-day week finished, Davy found the company improved 'out of sight' and took a far more professional attitude. In May 1974 he was promoted to the Birmingham store where he had, what he calls, two lucky breaks which brought him to the management's attention. 'When I took over at Birmingham, my brief was to clean up the store and get the furniture sales up. My first break was due to a television programme about Habitat for which they wanted to interview a typical store manager. Nobody in the company knew who I was and I was amazed then, and am even more now, that they allowed me to speak with no vetting. The only control was that my area manager was sitting around somewhere in the television building at the time. I was given three minutes in a half-hour programme and suddenly I was somebody in the company.

Terence and Michael Tyson both phoned to congratulate me the next morning.'

Break number two came when: 'I was still managing the store at the time of the bombings in Birmingham in 1974. They went off very close by. Over the next week the store opened and closed every hour with bomb threats. We had staff bursting into tears and some were not allowed to come to work by their mothers. But it did make our store the focus of attention within the company. I stayed there until Christmas 1974, when I was put in charge of the Wellingborough warehouse, national distribution and stock control.'

At that time it was felt that someone at the top of the company should have experienced as many of the company's separate fields of operation as possible. The warehouse had only been open for about a year and Geoff and his team were more or less camping in it – in a rough and ready pioneering way. The team was enthusiastic, committed and informal. 'I'd drive the forklift truck myself in the evenings,' he remembers. He worked closely with Bernard Higgins, the furniture buyer for Habitat, and through him Davy was gradually introduced to all the furniture suppliers. He was promoted to area manager for roughly half the Habitat shops, with about thirteen stores under him. When Bernard Higgins left the company, through poor health, Michael Tyson and Conran were concerned that a change of buyer should not weaken the allegiance of the suppliers. It was decided that Geoff Davy should become furniture buyer since he already knew them. Fifteen months later, David Phillips, lighting and accessories buyer, who had been at Woollands and then Habitat from the early days, left too. Davy took on his area in addition to furniture and was given two assistants. He found himself doing sixty per cent of the buying for Habitat.

David Phillips' decision to leave was the result of his desire to live in the lovely Sussex village of Alfriston where his mother had had a house for twenty-five years. 'My wife and I first thought of buying the village shop and post office there in the sixties but the owner was not inerested in selling. Then Terence bought Habitat back from Ryman and things looked up: there was masses of new buying to be done for the new shops and I thought no more about the village shop for five years. Then we heard the shop owner had been let down by an Australian who bought it, sight unseen, but was horrified when he saw it. We made an offer though not very seriously. But the owner accepted and we made the decision to go in twenty-four hours.'

However, there were other reasons behind his leaving. He explained to Conran and Michael Tyson that he was no longer too happy with his role at Habitat and felt his opinion was being overlooked too often. 'There were a lot of new men coming in. My buying had always been instinctive and I resented having to show it to a lot of people who didn't understand what I was doing. I could accept Terence's decisions, but was invariably irritated by other people making decisions which were not in their province.' Conran and Michael Tyson both asked him not to leave but within three weeks the Phillipses had sold their house and were on their way.

Habitat was continuing to expand at a fast rate. In 1975 stores were opened in Northampton (September) and Cardiff (November). In the same year in Europe, they opened in Montpellier (March) and Brussels (September). In March 1976 the Newcastle shop was founded and in early 1977 one opened in Wythenshawe, Manchester. And in October 1977 the leap was made over the Atlantic with the Conran store opening in Manhattan. Between then and 1980 new shops sprang up internationally at Edinburgh, Lille, Lyons, Strasbourg, Antwerp, Marseilles, New Rochelle, Les Halles, Hackensack (New Jersey), Milton Keynes, Hammersmith, Taplow, Manhasset, Washington, Southampton, Virginia, Hull and Velizy. Ten years after Habitat was demerged from Ryman the number of shops had risen from six, all in Britain, to forty-seven, with stores in France, Belgium, and the United States.

5 Going Abroad

TERENCE Conran had been deeply influenced by France. Like many of his contemporaries in the fifties, he appreciated the contrast it showed to Britain in its style, good living and general atmosphere. Unlike most of his contemporaries, he took aspects of what he liked and used it in his work – he absorbed the workings of a Paris restaurant before opening his Soup Kitchens; he enjoyed cooking in solid, French cookware, so he imported it for the first Habitat shop; and he was impressed by the impact of shopping in large French warehouses with the stock piled up to the ceiling, so he displayed Habitat merchandise in the same way.

The French were impressed by Habitat. His contact with the French retail market was initiated not by him but by an approach from a major French chain – Prisunic. Their chief stylist, Denise Fayolle, 'discovered' Habitat when she visited London in the sixties. Prisunic has been described as 'something between a supermarket and Marks and Spencer'. In 1967 their managing director was anxious to develop a new image for the stores. Denise Fayolle had seen what Conran had achieved and Prisunic decided to inject the same high standard of design.

When Prisunic launched its mail order catalogue in 1968, it included a range of products created by the Conran Design Group – they were an immediate success. French journalists and stylists praised the range – delighted to find something which broke with tradition and was fresh and inexpensive. A second Conran range was featured in the 1969 catalogue.

Francis Brugiere, Prisunic's furniture buyer, was impressed not only by Habitat goods, but by other aspects of the shops. He was a skilful retailer, with imagination and drive, and he had clear ideas about how he wanted to develop Prisunic's furniture departments. In the late sixties they were selling furniture only by mail order from a catalogue distributed through the shops. Brugiere felt this was not exploiting the full potential of the market. He suggested that they open a store in the centre of Paris, of about 550 square feet, to incorporate a furniture display. Prisunic hesitated. Frustrated and impatient, Brugiere approached Conran in 1969 and suggested he open a Habitat store in Paris. Conran was interested but not ready to move across the Channel.

By 1972, things had changed drastically. With Habitat out of Ryman and expanding, Conran felt they should consider going overseas. He was thinking of doing a feasibility study when he received a telephone call from a man he had never heard of but whose brash approach impressed him. Michael Likierman had been running a textile business with his father. When ICI bought them out in 1972, he was without a job. He informed Conran that what Habitat needed was a managing director – him. Conran assured Likierman he had a fine managing director but arranged to meet him. Likierman was a clever man and an able entrepreneur; he was also bilingual, in French. Conran explained that Habitat was considering opening a store in France and asked Likierman if he would be interested in doing the feasibility study. He was, and spent a year investigating possibilities in the retail markets of France. He found the market was ripe for Habitat. As a result, Habitat France was formed in 1973 with Michael Likierman as managing director and Francis Brugiere coming in as general manager and head of buying. Brugiere brought with him three colleagues from Prisunic. The first French Habitat store opened in Tour Montparnasse in Paris in September 1973 – during the same week as the King's Road store opened in London.

Habitat UK were deeply involved in the project and Conran spent about a year commuting between London and Paris. Zimmie Sasson, who had been with the first Habitat store where she had 'blossomed' when made a buyer, was now brought back into the company in order to co-ordinate merchandise for Britain and France. There were obviously going to be some major differences between what was sold in Britain and in France, but originally Zimmie Sasson took over to Paris one of everything sold in the British shops. There she went through it, piece by piece, with the French buyers and Francis Brugiere.

Obviously French cookware was available everywhere so that had to be dropped. She remembers that some of the chrome and glass furniture, by OMK, which did well in Britain, did not sell in France, and Habitat's popular 'overstuffed sofa' was a disaster there. Yet, at first glance, Habitat France seems almost identical to Habitat in Britain, and even today about sixty per cent of the products are the same. 'Obviously, the more products we can have in common the better, in practical terms,' says Francis Brugiere. The range for the whole group is built up from what is selected at four annual merchandise meetings attended by representatives from the British and French stores, and from the other countries where Habitat now has stores.

Conran's sister, Priscilla, moved to France in 1970, and Conran asked Zimmie Sasson to get her involved with Habitat. The two women got on well and their early collaboration on the first mail order catalogue for France was the beginning of a close relationship between Priscilla and Habitat. Zimmie Sasson recalls: 'Michael Nicholson took the photographs for the catalogue which was designed in London by Conran Associates.' The week it was launched, the French post office was on strike and it could not be mailed. 'The very first Habitat mail order catalogue in France was handed out to people who came into the store.'

The predicted turnover for Habitat France in the first year was F8 million. In fact they did better than that and reached F12 million. However, the company did not start making a profit for another three years; not until 1977. 'Unfortunately,' says Francis Brugiere, 'the rate of expansion put a strain on resources. Almost immediately we went from one shop to a small chain, with stores opening in two Paris suburbs. Then we took the decision to open another branch in central Paris and one in Brussels.' Habitat France had produced the necessary turnover and popularity to allow for this fast expansion from the beginning. Part of this success came from the company choosing the right moment to enter the French market, and part of it came from establishing a good management team.

The company continued to expand in Europe, opening branches in the high population areas of France and Belgium. In 1983, Habitat bought a branch of Maison de la Redoute, consisting of three large out-of-town stores, each one far larger than any other Habitat premises. The new stores were used to sell a much-expanded range of furniture and goods – sensible, value-for-money merchandise to attract a broader range of customers than the usual Habitat stores. The stores were renamed: Habitat Grand H.

In Britain it has taken retailers a long time to catch on to what Habitat is doing and try to steal ideas and follow suit. But in France, there were problems with this almost immediately, with companies not only copying the concept of Habitat but even using the name. Francis Brugiere says that, 'For a long time we were considered marginal, not to be taken seriously by the profession – they considered us fragile and trendy, good only for the young and intellectual. When things started to get serious there because of the economic crisis, they saw that the only store doing well was Habitat. One of the most outrageous copies was done by a discount store which opened a chain of Habitat-style stores in April

1983. They were called A + B and described themselves as a "kit market". The furniture was quite interesting and would have been worth selling over a long term or as an experiment. But they plunged in with four shops opening at the same time, and spending a huge amount on publicity and bad advertising. By June they were almost bankrupt.'

Habitat France runs in parallel with Habitat UK, closely linked but independent in certain areas including distribution, stock control and store management. Marketing, advertising and promotion are also run separately but a bridge is created between Habitat France and UK by a group marketing meeting held jointly every three months and attended by Conran. The French and Belgian mail order catalogue is produced at the same time and by the same people as the British one, with representatives and buyers cooperating on both sides of the Channel.

Michael Likierman left his job as managing director of Habitat France in 1976 and Michael Tyson briefly found himself commuting again between Paris and London, as managing director of Habitat UK and France. Francis Brugiere took over as managing director in France in 1976 and is now chief executive of the company. Michael Tyson followed up the changeover in Paris with an extended trip to New York – to conduct a feasibility study for opening Habitat in the USA.

Tyson arrived in New York in November 1976 and stayed for three weeks. He says, 'I was never in any doubt about this leap across the Atlantic but Terence, having pressed the start button, his finger lingered very close to the stop button for some time.' Conran says, 'Michael Tyson produced an over-optimistic feasibility study and I sounded a note of caution. In principle, I was very much in favour of opening in the USA.'

Having persuaded Conran, and the board, of his proposals, Tyson went straight back to New York to look for premises for a Habitat shop to open in Manhattan. One building which interested him was a vast dockside warehouse – 170,000 square feet. The space available was on the third floor, reached by elevators large enough to take trucks! It had no windows, and was generally regarded as too ambitious. In one of Manhattan's more derelict areas, between Lexington and Third Avenue on the lower east side, Citicorp of America were investing in a new tower block. This area of decaying tenements and seedy streets, with the Citicorp tower under construction in its midst, was certainly not an obvious location for a new business, let alone America's first Habitat.

However, the ability, of both Conran and Michael Tyson, to search out interesting properties and negotiate favourable terms for leasing, had long been an important factor in Habitat's success. Tyson's timing and instinct were right: the city was bankrupt, the area run down, so he was able to lease space in a very good, new building and at a very low rent, by New York standards. A three-level shopping area was planned for the tower and intended to incorporate many restaurants and food shops. Prospective tenants were not easy to come by in this area, so Conran was able to take out a twenty-year lease on two whole floors at $10 per square foot. There were to be no rent reviews and the air conditioning and heating were free.

Merchandise consultant, Pauline Dora, heard a rumour that Conran was planning to open a store in the USA and she says, 'I was determined to work for him. I rang up the *New York Times* and the British Council and eventually tracked him down. When I heard where he wanted to open I couldn't believe that anybody could be so stupid. There were no other retailers there at all. Customers would have to be pulled over from Bloomingdales, several blocks away.'

Michael Tyson and David Pasmore, Habitat UK's store director, travelled over to New York to supervise the creation of the store. They rented a small, dark office near the Citicorp construction site. An incomplete building provided the opportunity to ensure it was fitted as they required. The construction company fitters, restricted by union rules, proved to be more of a hindrance than a help. Habitat decided to go behind the construction company's, and the unions', backs and to do the fittings themselves. Lights, shelves and so on, arrived at the site labelled 'furniture' and as soon as the site was clear in the evening, they would get to work. Eventually the unions discovered what was going on but not until they had completed seventy-five per cent of the work, including assembling all the wooden fixtures. David Pasmore was told in plain terms: 'Keep doing this and we'll damage your goods and we'll damage you.'

Halfway through the preparations for the store a dock strike was threatened which brought a host of new decisions and question marks. They had to consider whether stock should be brought in from the UK through Canada or obtained in the USA.

Meanwhile, Pauline Dora, who had joined the company to take charge of buying, spent three weeks in Britain attending merchandising meetings and looking into the feasibility of taking stock for New York from the

British range and supplementing it with products specially suited to America. Expectations for the new store were high, greater than the event as it turned out, and she was told to order in quantities as great as for the King's Road store. A marketing meeting was held at Terence's country house, Barton Court, a few weeks before the New York opening. Conran was called to the telephone urgently and returned with terrible news. The name Habitat was the copyright of another company and could not be used. Two weeks before opening, Conran reluctantly agreed to change the name to Conran's.

It was early autumn in New York – very hot and very humid. In traditional Conran style, people were working around the clock and the project was beset by disaster. As the deadline approached, things became increasingly frantic with late-night meetings in hotel rooms, ending at maybe 10 pm with Conran calling the next one for 7 am. And when they weren't having meetings, they were working flat out, even before the change in name. That brought a burden of extra work because almost everything in the shop had Habitat written all over it.

Every Habitat label had to be removed and replaced, and all the signs had to be renewed, and every single price tag. Most of the goods were packaged ready for display. The glasses were wrapped in threes, in sleeves with Habitat printed across – they all had to be repacked. Every roll of wallpaper contained an instruction slip with Habitat printed top and bottom. A small team sat for hours, slitting the cellophane around each roll, changing the label on the instruction slips, then resealing the cellophane. Sheets, duvets and pillowcases had Habitat labels which were sewn into the bed linen. Each item was unwrapped, unfolded, labels replaced, refolded, rewrapped. Every light fitting had to be taken out of its box, labels unstuck, new labels stuck on, and the whole lot reboxed, 'and you know how difficult it is to get things back into boxes,' says someone who did it. A salesman from one of the lighting suppliers spent eighteen hours a day for several days setting up the entire lighting department and displaying not only his own lights but all the others as well. No one could help because they were all changing labels.

Pauline Dora will never forget the chicken bricks: 'Habitat had been stamped on the base of each of them before firing. We had to grind it off the bottom of every single chicken brick!' The heatwave continued and so did the disasters.

A week before opening the dock strike went ahead. Fifteen containers of merchandise were on their way to the store. The entire Christmas stock – toys, accessories, replacements for goods sold – stood idle on the dockside for two months. Pauline Dora received a message from Conran: 'Go out and buy in the US.' She did, chasing stock in competition with established US buyers but finding many products, such as toys, suitable for the store. In addition, Conran's pricing policy was strict and she did not have the buying power of her competitors. Somehow they provided a well-stocked store.

Conran 'took a big role' in the opening. He completed the accessorizing and design of the furniture floor himself, working, of course, through the night. Maurice Libby, with Habitat from the day it opened and still head of display in the UK, went over to New York to finalize the display. 'Terence came in saying, "What would you like me to do?" He had a strong feeling he had to make a personal statement in New York. The shop bore his name and it was a highly exciting new market with great potential. It had to be right. It was the first time for a long time that we'd seen Terence working on the shop floor with us.'

The list of disasters seemed never ending. One of the final ones occurred when the store was just about ready: the air conditioning was turned on for the first time and blew dust across everything.

Conran's New York opened on Terence's birthday, 4 October 1977.

'The biggest blitz' of publicity was organized by New Yorker Michael Steinberg, 'who knows everybody'. Practically every major newspaper and magazine wrote about Conran's – it was the hot story, the most exciting retail event of the year in Manhattan, possibly the country. The *New York Times* contained four colour pages on the store and the *New Yorker* magazine wrote: 'Here is a shop with empathy for the shoppers; wallpaper paste with wallpaper, one soup bowl or a set.'

Pauline Dora says, 'Terence handled the press expertly, he has the personality and ability to communicate. They loved his accent and the way he'd sit, a little unkempt, a little sloppy. Anyway, New York is an event- and media-oriented city and nothing else important was happening. People were very curious about the building – which was originally intended to use solar heat.

'The night we opened, Terence unlocked the tills and sold a lot of merchandise and books – he doesn't believe you can have a free opening party.'

Everybody who came to the new store was impressed but bemused. People asked: 'What *is* it?' The whole concept was quite fresh to them since stores in New York are generally highly specialized. The furniture was quite new. 'I don't think there was another store selling blond wood which is Conran's stock in trade,' says Pauline Dora. 'And the quick assembly concept – buying in cartons and assembling at home – did not exist in New York at the time.' At first it seemed the concept would not catch on but quick assembly furniture now sells very well in all the Conran stores in the US A.

Sales were disappointing initially – about thirty to forty per cent down on what had been expected. But for the first year the store was pioneering. Construction continued on the Citicorp building for some while after Conran's opened and the proposed shopping centre inside did not come into existence for over a year. Michael Tyson had found a building in New Rochelle, near New York, which would provide a location for offices and warehouse facilities which were desperately needed. He thought a store would do well there, and the building was cheap. There was room to establish the mail order company for America there as well. The plans went ahead and a neon sign erupted from the top of the building implying that Conran's owned the whole gigantic thing – people were impressed.

Pauline Dora categorically refused 'in her inimitable way' to go to New Rochelle. It was a twenty-minute journey from Manhattan but New Yorkers do not like to commute, especially out of the city. She left the company for a while after two years with Conran's and set up a Marimekko shop in partnership with a friend. When Michael Tyson, who had continued to run the US business while remaining a member of the main board, left in January 1982, at the time of the acquisition of Mothercare in Britain, Pauline Dora returned as vice president in charge of merchandising. She became executive vice president of the company at the end of 1982.

The American stores took much longer to take off than had been anticipated. It was six years before they began to make a profit but by the end of 1982 there were nine stores there, a flourishing mail order catalogue and sales for the year ending June 1982 were $22 million.

Pauline Dora has been highly influential: 'I admire Terence tremendously, but he spent very little time in the US and I disagreed very much with the marketing. I always believed Habitat could work in the States but you have to adapt a concept to a country. Perhaps the biggest mistake – or learning experience – was when Terence tried to duplicate the Habitat concept exactly here in America. Had he been over here more, he would have picked up the subtle differences which were so important because he is an extraordinary merchant. We've had to change the English tumblers which are not big enough to take ice. Terence says we Americans drink out of buckets. We sell a toast rack but nobody knows what it is, so shoppers use it as a letter rack. Sofas are bigger in America and they buy a lot of sofa beds because apartments here are so small. We are more gift oriented than in the UK, so that's a bigger department, and not quite so basic, a little more fun.'

A large proportion of the merchandise for the US is brought over from Europe but much of it is specially geared to the American way of life. Some European goods simply do not work or sell in the US and most of the upholstered furniture sold there is also made there.

The expansion to Europe and then to the US was a success for Conran and had clear advantages in helping to keep the company buoyant during crises. The financial crisis in Britain during the late seventies was made less bleak for Habitat because Habitat France was making good profits. Similarly, hard times in France in 1983 meant smaller profits there, but US and UK profits helped to bolster the Habitat business.

With Europe and America established, Conran looked east and entered the Japanese retail market in 1982. This time the whole approach and installation into a new market was quite different. Habitat formed a joint company with the prestigious Seibu group – a large chain of department stores and leisure centres throughout Japan, with hotel and railway interests.

Negotiations between Conran and Seibu started in 1980 after Oliver Cregory, Chris Turner and Geoff Davy accompanied Conran on a visit to Japan to initiate the project, and from then on the Japanese came to London to see Habitat at work. Teams of up to twenty of them would attend Habitat meetings, particularly merchandising meetings, and they returned 'again and again'. Joint ventures and franchising were both new to Habitat but the management team could not see how else to approach the Japanese market. The system of marketing and management, the way of life, is so different there that it was felt that Habitat could only enter Japan through a Japanese company. Chris Turner, Habitat UK's chief executive, and his colleagues did find cultural problems at first, but the Seibu team 'dedicated so many resources and so much enthusiasm to the project that they almost became Habitat', says John Stephenson.

Francis Brugiere, of Habitat France, attended many of the meetings during the period of negotiations with the Japanese: 'There were more of them than there were of us at some meetings. They all kept completely straight faces, no sign of enthusiasm and yet when they set up the shops they were the spitting image of the Habitats in Europe. They had produced items and put them on the shelves which they could only have seen on the drawing boards in the Habitat design department, and they had them for sale before they were in production in Europe. The merchandise is almost the same for Japan – most of the furniture is made seven per cent smaller, but the kitchenware is completely different.'

After two years of negotiations and preparations, six Habitat-within-Seibus, and one separate shop, to act as a flagship, opened in Japan in October 1982. Conran had entered one of the most difficult markets in the world for western retailers. By 1983, the joint venture with Seibu had achieved eleven Habitat outlets in Japan. Habitat had a nominal one-per-cent equity stake in the venture, with an option to increase it to thirty per cent. The main income for Habitat comes from the royalty payments on goods sold. In the three months trading in 1982, royalties amounted to $68,000 and are expected to rise to at least $1.5 million per annum in the following five years.

Habitat entered Japan at a time when Japanese design, particularly of clothes and cars, is at a peak of popularity in the west. The venture has provided an excellent opportunity for Habitat to get access to Japanese products at a time when their ceramics, cutlery and kitchen equipment are in great demand. Although Japanese business methods, which include many middle people to be dealt with, make it difficult for buyers to get to direct sources for products, Habitat is now buying goods from Seibu suppliers and is confident the range will do well in Europe. The cleanness of line, simplicity of decoration, and attractive texture of Japanese objects seem perfectly matched to Habitat's own traditional approach to houseware.

6 Design

CONRAN was a designer before he became involved in manufacturing furniture and then in retailing through Habitat. It is something in which he has always been obsessionally interested and an area of his work which he regards as central to everything else. He set up the Conran Design Group in 1955, when he was struggling to become a furniture manufacturer. Through the group he continued his work as an interior designer, product and furniture designer, exhibition designer, fabric designer and so on. It was undoubtedly one of the most successful of his early enterprises and in troubled times, the design group often helped to finance other areas of the company.

That original group stayed behind when Habitat was bought back from Ryman's, so he wasted no time in establishing a new design team. Conran Associates was founded before Habitat was officially demerged from Ryman's in January 1971. He had used the first design group as a part of his business and in order to gain design commissions from outside clients. This he intended to continue – Conran Associates was to be responsible for styling the new Habitat shops during the hectic period of expansion. They were to design the catalogue for the developing mail order business, and play a central role in product development for the shops. They were also to be at the forefront of other design work, doing whatever was required for clients around the world.

Design continued to be a central axis in the Habitat organization. Habitat was an expression of a certain design appreciation and an understanding of style. The look of the shops and what they sold was the result of a series of decisions in which design considerations were fundamental. Although Conran himself sees his approach to design as 'ad hoc', its integration into the organization is far from haphazard. It ensures the Habitat 'look' is never stale and with a prestigious and highly respected design group within the organization, Conran makes sure the ideas keep flowing, and that he has a creative source from which to draw inspiration and practical knowledge. Design is not a precious commodity for Conran, it must work and enhance, not merely be appreciated in the abstract.

Habitat merchandise is not just a collection of nice-looking things.

Their selection is based on simplicity, comfort, practicality, usefulness, visual ease, attractiveness and, above all, commonsense. The products, the look of the shops and the general atmosphere, reflect a certain attitude to life and a way of living.

Conran says, 'If you go into a shop with a mishmash of styles and nothing cohesive, you confuse the customer. You have Scandinavian pine here, G-Plan and reproduction there; nobody's selling anything with confidence; there is no feeling that "This is our style, like it or leave it". Our confidence and style are convincing to people who shop with us.' It is achieved through a carefully maintained balance between Conran's own instinct, observation and clearly defined taste and the input of the enthusiastic, well-trained and decisive people on the buying and design teams.

Oliver Gregory, who became a top board director of Habitat, was put in charge of Conran Associates. He was joined by David Wren, Guy Fortescue and Stafford Cliff. Almost immediately they found far too much work to cope with. Michael Tyson was expanding Habitat fast and the mushrooming stores had to be designed. Commissions were coming in constantly for work for outside clients in Britain and around the world.

Habitat shops required immediate attention and in 1972 David Salter was brought in to take responsibility for co-ordinating the design of the new stores. The number of shops doubled in a year, and he worked on twelve stores in twelve months. David Salter had trained as an architect, then worked with George Drew Dunn in the sixties, on large building projects such as hospitals and universities. He worked for another firm of architects, Yorke Rosenberg Mardall, and then for IBM. Despite IBM, he did not see himself as a big-company man. 'Conran Associates, the design group, had only been in existence fifteen months when I joined and was still quite small.'

His brief was clear: to create the Habitat ambience and provide the environment in which the merchandise would look most appealing, and to avoid creating anything too luxurious, expensive or alienating for customers. The pattern had been set with the early stores, and the overall effect was to remain informal. 'Certainly, if you were to compare an original store with a present day one, you would recognize them as the same animals, but if you analysed the materials, the fittings, lighting and so on, you would see that in fact everything has changed,' he says.

65

Tina Ellis was one of several young designers who worked with him. She joined in 1973, when in her early twenties, and stayed until 1982. She was working as a designer when she applied for the job and remembers her interview vividly: 'It was pouring with rain and my portfolio, containing a cardboard project, was falling to bits. I'd ripped my tights by nervously dropping a cigarette on them. David Salter looked at my work but suggested I should come back and see Oliver Gregory. I thought I was getting a bum deal, but I came back. For the second time I was kept waiting. Eventually I found Oliver Gregory with his feet on his office table and a cigar in his mouth. He flicked through my stuff for a couple of minutes and then offered me a sum of money. He said, "I suppose you want to discuss it with your husband." I was furious, felt I'd been dismissed completely. As I left he called out, "Tina, *do* come." '

She joined in January 1973. 'I can remember the day, it's printed on my mind forever. Everything was being done at breakneck speed and on a minimal budget. Douglas Cooper, who I was supposed to be working under, was away. I was expected to get on with things on my own. I was helplessly miserable for a few days; Habitat was expanding and nobody had time for anything. Even when Douglas came back, he was distracted. He was having problems at home. We were laying out plans for the King's Road store at the time and I was copying amended drawings for electrical sockets. When Oliver Gregory checked one of them he found a mistake and wrote a particularly rude word in big letters all over the drawing. I didn't even know what it meant and wanted to cry. When I plucked up the courage to tell the others, they all laughed and said, "Oh, that's just Oliver." That epitomizes him – he could do that and two minutes later be utterly charming.' As another ex-colleague says, 'Oliver is a very, very charming man but always lords you around.'

Designers were thrown in at the deep end and found themselves with responsibilities they would usually have had to wait some time for. Stores of very different sizes and shapes were opening. Tour Montparnasse opened the same week as King's Road, and the design team would move on from these to very different buildings in Romford, say, or Kingston. Tina Ellis remembers: 'We had about ten goes at making a design manual, but I rate it as a compliment that we never succeeded. We were always looking at new materials and new possibilities.'

In the early-seventies shops, materials used included white painted brick walls, dark-brown quarry tiles for the floors, slatted ceilings made from rough timber painted white, and display shelves of timber or white

66

formica supported by brick panels also painted white. The lighting was a battery of heat-producing spotlights. Smells of spices and basketware pervaded the atmosphere and anyone who was not already seduced into buying was also bombarded with background music. Those early stores were usually between 15,000 and 11,000 square feet.

An equivalent shop in the 1980s will be at least 20,000 square feet, and extensive adjoining parking facilities are essential. Materials used today are different. The walls are still likely to be plain white brick, and floors will still be tiles, but not rustic quarry tiles, more likely smaller, machined, light beige, ceramic tiles. Ceilings are no longer rough timber slats – they had a tendency to fall down and fire regulations often excluded them. Now, there may be no false ceiling at all and where there is it will be metal slats, used vertically, or a gridded material known as Formalux. The look is much more machine-finished than of old.

A special system is used to hide service pipes or other clutter, and this also incorporates the lighting system. Spotlights are used with more control – as highlights against a sophisticated system of low energy, economic ambient fluorescent lighting. The systems used for display have changed drastically. The original shelving suspended between brick panels proved very inflexible. The height could not be adjusted and they were permanently fixed. Special units designed for glass or linens could not be used for other products. Many experiments and developments took place before a suitable system was found. It is constructed of timber and completely flexible, so that it may be moved around the store, used for a range of products and has infinitely adjustable shelf heights.

In 1976, Conran established a new design group at Barton Court, his home in Berkshire, thirty miles from London. Conran Associates were extremely busy designing the shops and doing all manner of outside work. He wanted a small team, close to him, to concentrate on product design and development. The new studios went into the stables and those chosen to work there had to leave London and live locally. Oliver Gregory was one of them. His second marriage was in difficulties so he was attracted to the idea of living in the country and agreed to run the group. Conran himself spent a major part of his time at Barton Court, working with his secretary in a specially constructed office. Michael Wickham, his old photographer friend from the workshop days, joined him to spend three years building furniture prototypes, commuting from his own country home in the adjoining county.

'The setting was idyllic,' says Oliver Gregory, 'but it proved in the long run to be too isolated. As far as I was concerned, it was just at the right moment that the Habitat Mothercare merger took place in 1981. It meant Terence could not spend so much time away from London and we needed a bigger design group to cope with the extra Mothercare work.'

In 1981, Habitat Mothercare Group Design was formed. Like Conran Associates, they worked from the Neal Street offices but were quite separate. John Stephenson headed the new design group, and under him were Oliver Gregory, who moved back to London, Conran's sister Priscilla, David White, Alan McDougall and Malcolm Riddell. A number of other designers were involved, including Conran's eldest son, Sebastian, who was made responsible for much of the Mothercare hardware, including pushchairs.

The new Habitat Mothercare Group Design is responsible for all shop design for the group of companies – Oliver Gregory is again in charge of this – leaving Conran Associates free to work only for outside clients. Shop design now includes not only all Habitat, Richard Shops and Mothercare stores, but also any new acquisitions which have included, so far, Heal's, in Tottenham Court Road, and now to be the group's headquarters as well as containing a Habitat, Mothercare, NOW and a new Heal's shop. Group Design will be there, alongside group advertising, fashion design and the photographic studios and so on. The administrative offices are situated on the top floor. Sections of the company, concerned with projects outside the main group, remain in Neal Street in Covent Garden. These include Conran Associates and Conran Advertising, and, of course, the Neal Street Restaurant.

Despite the move and reforming of the Barton Court group, an expansion of the design group and a splitting away of Conran Associates, Conran himself keeps in close touch with what is going on in the design field of his company. 'I keep my sanity by being constantly involved in the creative feel and look of things. It is the part of the business I enjoy far and away the most, and I often feel this sort of ad hoc way of working, a kind of design shorthand that we use, is not ideal, but it works.' He has a continuous flood of ideas, not just for Conran Associates, but for the Habitat Mothercare Group Design as well, and for all his shops including NOW and Richard Shops. Reading books or magazines, he tears out pages or rings items of interest, then passes them on. He still has a major influence on the design side, pouring over drawings with designers and spending time on the most minute details. When a new restaurant was planned for Heal's, he was involved in the initial discussions with Oliver Gregory; he checked the first drawings and took part in every decision, such as the colour of the wood, the type of chairs to be used, the colour of the tablecloths and accessories, the difference in decoration of the tables between lunch and tea, and even the display of the cakes and salads. This is what he has always enjoyed doing most.

In its first year, Habitat Mothercare Group Design created over five hundred new products for Habitat alone. It took them just over eighteen months to revamp all the Mothercare stores and a considerable proportion of the Mothercare merchandise. Separate teams are responsible for different areas within the group: the product team has a workshop for producing prototypes; the interiors studio concentrates on the stores; there is a catalogue studio; an advertising studio; and the newer fashion team works on clothes for Mothercare and the more recently acquired Richard Shops, as well as the new NOW chain of stores for young people. Conran's second son, fashion designer Jasper, has contributed to this side of the design output.

Conran Associates continue their work on interiors, product design, packaging graphics and advertising for large and small clients all over the world. One of their most important clients has been the British Airports Authority. They have undertaken an enormous project for them in the eighties with work on the new Terminal Two at Gatwick Airport in Sussex. It is a seven-year project and the designer needs to meet with representatives every week. They are working with architects Yorke Rosenberg Mardall and the terminal is due for completion in 1987. In addition, Conran Associates have been retained as house designers for Terminal Three at Heathrow, where they are called in as work is necessary on the tax-free shop or the land side buffet. Other recent work has included interiors for the Next chain of fashion stores, owned by Hepworth; Jean Jeannie leisure clothes shops; the London Electricity Board shops; and Lord Carrington's office at the General Electric Company. They have worked on the Sarma Penney hypermarkets in Belgium, part of the giant J.C. Penney organization in America; on Miss Selfridge stores; and on product designs for the House of Fraser, for various forms of houseware; and for Marks and Spencer.

Car interior design has now become a speciality. Conran Associates have designed for Renault. For Fiat they have done the Habitat Panda, of which five hundred were put into production with colours and materials and other special features which made it unique. At present they are working on the future styling of dashboards, not intended for immediate production.

David Salter still heads the group and says, 'A lot of our work is done abroad. For instance, we are doing holiday site development in Sardinia's Costa Smeralda for the Aga Khan. We have designed a group of offices for the organizers of the scheme: they're glorified estate agents really, and pretty high-powered salesmen, working from what looks like Churchill's war room where they each have a work station and use symbols for each of the yachts which they move around like tanks, on a map.'

They have work in Curaçao, in the Dutch Antilles, where they are European consultants for holiday/business areas, including short-let offices for an 'offshore tax haven'. The scheme is a very big one, sponsored by a Dutch merchant bank in consortium with a mining company who have excavated part of a large mountain to make it all possible. Conran Associates is part of the design team which also includes a Dutch civil engineering company.

In Botswana, a developing African country with a young diamond-mining industry, they have worked on the interior of an office-equipment sales business started by a typewriter mechanic who went out there to work and found he could stay, and wanted to.

In Britain, they are rehabilitating a twenty-year-old shopping centre without much character, they intend to put in covered aisles, co-ordinated street information signs, and decent, modern lighting.

In product design one of their triumphs has been the Crayonne range of plastic houseware – which continues to be highly successful and greatly admired. As a result of their work for Crayonne, the group have been commissioned by Timothy Whites, Marks and Spencer and Woolworths to do plastic houseware ranges. They have a good relationship with Sony, where Conran Associates has a strong impact on European and Central American products.

Stafford Cliff joined the Conran Design Group in 1968 as an office junior when it was to be found in Hanway Place, off Oxford Street. He fetched coffee and worked in the studio when he could. 'That was when Fletcher Forbes and Gill were just starting to make a name for themselves, when David Gentleman was putting stamps on the map with his new designs, and the British in general were establishing themselves with a high reputation for quality graphic design.' Working from a tiny room,

Terence Conran the young designer. The year was 1952 and he was twenty-one.
He is seen here at an exhibition, in Simpson of Piccadilly, of his designs and
constructions.

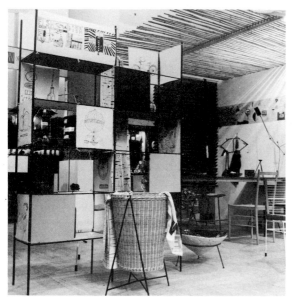

The 1952 exhibition showed Conran's 'ideas and objects for the home'. Included are some of his early fabric and furniture designs, drawings and objects, creating a stark and modern environment.

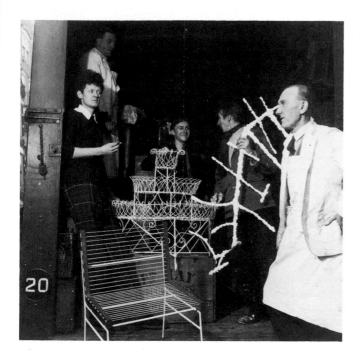

In the early 1950s Conran was making unusual metal constructions for the home in his workshop and is seen here helping to unload some of them.

Conran seated in the classic cane chair on a metal frame which was one of the items he sold from his first showroom, opened in 1953 in the Piccadilly Arcade.

One of the hallmarks of Habitat is the bold and imaginative displays inside the stores. A vast pile of chicken bricks (*left*) almost reaches the ceiling and is complemented in tone and texture by the stacked basketware behind. Brightly coloured sag-bags are best shown in piles (*above*) while the equally vibrant tones of ethnic rugs make an eye-catching display on a rack. Even pottery can be bunched as is shown by this display of mugs (*right*) offering contrast to the neat rows of handsome teapots.

A Habitat window
incorporated a rope ladder
in a display of basketware
and rugs (*left*). Inside the
Kingston-upon-Thames
store (*below*) kitchen
utensils almost overflow
from the shelves.

The many faces of Habitat (*clockwise from above*):
the classic logo against tiles; an open frontage at
Hammersmith; a converted nineteenth-century church in
Tunbridge Wells; the Citicorp building, New York;
the Montparnasse store in France.

Habitat offers a complete and co-ordinated range and the fabrics have always been an integral part of this. Wallpapers are printed to the same designs and fabrics used for upholstered furniture can often be bought separately. This allows customers to create their own co-ordinating curtains, bedspreads or other features to match their Habitat furniture. Linda Brill designed 'Fruit Orchard' (*left*), which first appeared in 1975, and Susan Collier's delightful 'Egyptian Birds' (*below*) was part of the 1977 range.

he did graphics for Bulmer's Cider, Harvey's Bristol Cream, Peter Dominic, and Mowlem – who had commissioned a new corporate identity. Although at the head of the graphics side of Conran Associates, and its Creative Director, Stafford Cliff also involves himself in interior design projects and does work on new products. His team recently produced a range of bedlinens for Dan River, a big American textile firm. The range is called the Conran Millenium Collection and has world-wide distribution. Cliff is responsible for running the project and art directing the photographs for the brochure, and originating designs for 'the year 2000, updating them from year to year, so that they are not just a passing fad.'

Cliff was also responsible for the design of *The Housebook*, Conran's first venture into books, which was followed by *The Kitchen Book* and *The Bed and Bath Book*. He is a director of the new publishing company set up by Conran with Paul Hamlyn of Octopus in late 1983. He is also an author, having worked on *French Style* with Suzanne Slesin of the *New York Times*, published in 1982, and on *English Style*, published in 1984, both by Thames and Hudson.

David Salter was appointed managing director of Conran Associates in 1983. He employs between eighty and ninety people on the design side, and a marketing group in addition to this, whose job is to get new business. 'I have always said that marketing has a key role to play in design consultancy. But once the project is running, the designer should be in control. The system doesn't always work because some designers are not so good at the business aspects of running a project. And with some clients, and some designers, it is necessary to have a design manager. But we do not want to have "acount handlers". The strength of the whole organization lies in its deep commitment to design. A lot of people suppose (I think mistakenly) that there is a "Conran Style". There was, certainly, in the late sixties and early seventies. Clients came to us then because they wanted to be part of that style, but when things became more difficult in the early and middle seventies, and there was not so much cash around, we had to be more aggressive about finding work. And the generation which was growing up saw a wider opportunity and stopped clinging on to the one product or look, and thought more philosophically about design.'

Conran Associates has a Paris office and a smaller design group has been set up in New York, a branch of Habitat Mothercare Group Design, with an office in the Citicorp building. It meets the design needs of the

Conran's shop there and creates the mail order catalogue for America. The US stores are actually designed in Britain, which can be difficult at times given the differences in building laws, techniques, traditions and available materials. However, the intention has always been to maintain a coherent store design wherever they are located. The American design team assist and work is carried out with an American architect.

A developing policy within Conran's company as a whole is to link up with other specialized firms in order to provide a comprehensive and expert service in the design field for all clients. In 1983, Conran Associates got together with surveyors Michael Laurie and partners to form a venture, Conran Laurie, specializing in renovation and refurbishment of older shopping centres.

7 How It Works

WHEN Habitat was created, Conran's organization was as informal and instinctive as the shops themselves – the first store is remembered almost as a club. Conran liked to be there on Saturdays and watch people meeting in his Habitat and 'smiling because they were there'.

Each of the staff had a feeling of being involved in every aspect of what was going on. 'We had a say, with Terence, in the selection of merchandise and stock control, and we did absolutely everything ourselves, even the cleaning.' It was, as so many people have repeated, the most fun place to work, but even then there was an underlying feeling that things would have to become rather more professional. Habitat has come a long way since then. The first shop in the Fulham Road had a turnover of £65,000 in its first year. The King's Road store, today just one in a major international chain, now takes that amount on the first day of a sale. Even allowing for inflation in the last twenty years, it is an indication of a phenomenal development.

When Habitat merged with Ryman in 1968 it was a small concern with five stores. The first area manager had been appointed that year. Over the next two years, during which Conran found himself taking a back seat in the running of Habitat, his top staff became depleted and the company was generally demoralized. John Mawer, managing director of Habitat at the time of the merger, left after being involved in a serious car crash. Michael Tyson, managing director of the factory at Thetford where Conran was manufacturing furniture, left in 1969. David Phillips, who had been brought in as buyer for the first shop, and Peter Hope, director of stores, used to joke that it was only a matter of time before their turn would come along to be managing director of Habitat. The company in fact had seven managing directors in two years. Throughout the Ryman era, 1968–70, there were only two working directors on the Habitat side. They always did their best to hold the company together but against difficult odds – no new stores, except the one in Brighton, were opened, and the existing ones began to stagnate. Ryman centralized all the functions of the business: wages, accounts, stock control, and so on. When the split came, and Conran bought Habitat out, he lost all that management organization and machinery.

He had one top buyer but no financial director. He did not even have an office from which to operate.

A base was his first priority when he had decided to leave Ryman in 1970. He soon arranged to rent a large building in Neal Street, Covent Garden, owned by Christina Smith. Michael Tyson came back to be managing director of Habitat and from 1970-1972 the company found the key financial people it needed and enlarged the buying team. Tyson expanded as quickly as possible to increase turnover and buying power. Gradually, the organization began to build a tight structure and a co-ordinated, professional pattern of operating. Today it is expertly run, with the complex structure required to maintain a very large business. Conran remains at the centre of his 'empire' but he stresses that it is, and always has been, a team effort, and he is one member of that team.

MERCHANDISE

How do Habitat, and the other stores owned by Conran's organization, decide which products to sell? A buying brief is decided for a period, and perhaps for years ahead, at an orientation meeting. Ideally they take place once a year, but more usually every eighteen months or so. Their purpose is to give the buyers a direction so that they know the type of products to look for in terms of range, image, price, style, colour and presentation.

These meetings are attended by Conran, the chief buyers and the chief designers.

They try to look at the merchandising with fresh eyes and discuss what it should consist of, which areas they should concentrate on, which styles they want to develop, what colour trends are to be. It is all considered in the broadest terms, yet these are not vague, policy discussions. They will try to reach a concensus of opinion and make positive decisions which can be followed by direct action.

For example, some years ago there was an orientation meeting at which the Basics Range, of simple, inexpensive furniture, was decided upon and defined. At a meeting in 1983, the team classified for themselves the newly introduced City, First Home and Country ranges, deciding the categories of merchandise for each range, how particular products might be presented, and precisely the sorts of products required for each range. Orientation meetings are a forum for new projects, ideas and inspirations.

It is rare these days for Conran to dictate what is to be done. As one buyer says: 'It's not Terence saying, "I see such and such as the way we should go." We all put in ideas all the time.' If Conran [known as TOC – Terence Orby Conran] does have particularly strong views about something: 'Everybody knows what's going on. "Oh, this is a TOC special, let's give it a try," we say. Sometimes his ideas turn out to be fantastic successes, and all of us are prepared to admit it. If, however, it doesn't sell, it comes straight out of the range. But not every product can be a bestseller – its all part of the creative merchandising. When a product put forward by a particular buyer is a dismal failure, TOC won't condemn it out of hand. "Well, that wasn't one of your better decisions was it?" he's likely to say.'

By the end of the meeting, when decisions have been summarized, the buyers have a clear brief and are ready to start searching for new products and, at the same time, looking at ways of undating existing ones. The orientation meetings are important for the buyers and designers. It gives them an idea of the style of the new range and stimulates them into thinking in new ways and provides renewed motivation to them for finding more and varied products.

They may discover products at trade fairs, on a tour of factories in a certain country, or through businesses which approach the team with particular items. On some occasions they will find a manufacturer who has no products suitable for Habitat but who does have a particular manufacturing capability which Habitat could use. There may be a feeling that the factory is right to take the volume of work and make the quantity of products required at an acceptable price, but that it requires some design input. The buyer will brief the Habitat Mothercare Group Design, in particular the design studio, to come up with a product which will fill a gap in the market and can be produced at the factory. Occasionally, the studio itself will come up with ideas for a product or a range and suggest it to the buyers.

During the creative period for new products, Conran and his team hold a working meeting and a merchandising meeting. The working meeting follows up from the orientation meeting. Here the buyers and Priscilla Carluccio, Conran's sister who is now a director of Habitat Mothercare Group Design, stage a sort of dress rehearsal for the merchandising meeting. They will do things such as eliminate duplication of products between France, the USA and the UK, or they might reject a product they feel is excellent but not feasible to do at that time. It may contain the germ of an idea which can be used later. The buyers will present suggestions on materials, prices and styles for the design studio, and the designers will then suggest various propositions, discuss manufacturers and begin making the detailed drawings of products.

The product is finalized only after further, detailed discussions. Decisions are then made on packaging and how it is to be presented. The graphic designers will now be briefed. All this happens long before it appears in the shops – maybe a year.

An original member of staff, now a director, says, 'These days I find looking at new product proposals the hardest thing. We are looking at products, nine months ahead and we have to bear in mind what Terence has said about the trend for the year.' His staff consider Conran to be sometimes several steps ahead of the rest of the world. A colleague describes how Terence insisted one year that red be the basic Habitat colour. They found it difficult to sell at first, 'though it was going like hot cakes a year later. Terence does lead the fashion element.'

Merchandise meetings establish specifically which products shall be included in the Habitat range over the next six-month period. Two merchandise meetings take place each year for each type of product: lighting, furniture, cabinet/upholstery, wall coverings, textiles, linens, floor coverings, kitchenware, tableware, toys and accessories. Conran always attends, as does Priscilla Carluccio. Also there are the managing directors of Habitat UK, Habitat France, Conran's USA, Seibu Japan, the sales directors, marketing directors, buying directors and the buyers for each area of merchandise. Each buyer presents his/her suggestions for which products should go into the Habitat range. These may be existing products from manufacturers, products slightly altered to suit Habitat, or products designed exclusively for the group. Any products presented must already have been checked for suitability for mass production and the meeting decides if it should go in the range as it is, if it requires further modification of colour, design or materials, and if it is the right price. Conran has confidence in his team to make the right decisions but very occasionally he may refuse outright to include a product others recommend, or he may insist that something is included in the range despite opposition. He is far more likely to suggest a final touch or change: that a teacup needs to be a millimetre lower (a favourite criticism), or would be nicer if it were a slightly darker shade of grey. Everyone respects his eye for detail.

Habitat have the ability to search out the products they want, and if they cannot find them being made, to create a prototype in their design studio and then look for a manufacturer. New designs can create problems for manufacturers and difficulties arise if they do not appreciate what the new product is or do not feel any enthusiasm for it. However, the group is moving more and more in the direction of having their goods specially designed and manufactured for their market.

Seeking out good products from manufacturers, and ones particularly suited to the Habitat range, has never been easy. David Phillips, chief buyer for many years in the early days, says, 'We were the first house furnishing retailers ever to take an active role in adapting and establishing products specially for our market. No retailer had gone out deliberately to get manufacturers to make for them what they wanted to sell to the public. I remember visiting factories, particularly pottery and glass companies, where they would show us the usual run-of-the-mill stuff. Then I'd catch sight of a simple pot which they wouldn't have thought of showing us and which was far more exciting than their other produce. Reps who came round would offer the "saleable stuff" first, at the top of their suitcases, but we could often find just what we were looking for underneath all that.'

Today, Habitat continues to search out the simple products with an unusual slant. Alison Richards, buying director, recently visited a garden pottery which make goods for a garden centre in Ireland. 'He showed us his pots and then, as an afterthought, he mentioned a large tandoori pot he had developed with his Indian partner – designed so that tandoori cooking can be done at home. We forgot the pots and discussed the tandoori. Like the wok, which Habitat sold so successfully when it was available nowhere else but small Chinese shops in Soho, it is a very interesting idea for the kitchen department. The tandoori has potential for complementary books on Indian cookery, and could provide marketing ideas such as joint promotions with Indian spice companies, and competitions with Air India and Taj Hotels and so on.'

Alison Richards joined Habitat in 1979, from Timothy Whites, as buyer for toys and accessories. She had made contact when Conran Associates were working on a range of kitchen products for Timothy Whites. Conran told her later: 'I saw you at the meeting and thought you looked bright.' A year after she joined, the kitchenware buyer left and Alison took over that department as well, with two assistants. In August 1983 she became buying director, taking over from Geoff Davy when he left to become managing director of Heal's.

PRODUCT DESIGN

Priscilla Carluccio, a director of Habitat Mothercare Group Design, works closely with the people in the design studio, pointing them in the right direction and keeping the team together and on the Habitat path. Their purpose is to serve the design needs of the company and they are discouraged from producing speculative ideas. All projects come from general discussions and briefs from the buyer as to what is needed – where the gaps are in the range. There are other areas of design – such as wallpaper, fabrics, floor coverings and graphic products – where there are not gaps as such but where designs need to be renewed or refreshed each year.

The studio's brief originates from the orientation, working and merchandising meetings. Without undermining the work of the designers, they are told in general terms what is required in the way of shape, colour and texture. A buyer may suggest that the range includes plenty of stainless steel cutlery but none with plastic handles – so why not design some. The studio will usually produce a proposal or a series of possible alternatives. The buyers may accept one of these or ask for some reworking of the idea. Then it goes to the stage of working drawings and is discussed again before the finished drawings or prototypes are handed over to the manufacturer selected by the buyer.

MARKETING

Within the company structure there is a marketing committee which is taken very seriously indeed. They consider the promotion of the products well in advance of them reaching the shops, and they carefully control every aspect of marketing. Tony Maynard is marketing director for Habitat UK. He joined in 1978 when the company had a crying need for someone to take control of marketing. Maynard had been marketing manager with Rank Hovis McDougall and handled the promotion of their packaged food products such as Bisto, and Cerebos and Saxa salt. He was ready to move out of that area and the retail experience offered by Habitat presented a creative challenge to him.

His initial task was to provide a marketing plan and create a focus for marketing within the company. The evaluation process was both interesting and complicated, and very worthwhile. Maynard took over responsibility for the catalogue, advertising, promotions, mail order administration and dispatch. He also takes an active role in display decisions, and has become involved in the in-house credit card scheme with the financial department under John Beer. The marketing department is now an important section of the group.

Habitat's orginal philosophy was to bring simple, modern, brightly coloured, practical, well-designed and moderately-priced furniture and houseware to a young upmarket audience. In the sixties it was undertaking pioneering retailing, with a small but passionate following. Today the basic principles have not changed but the market has become more sophisticated and the audience for Habitat is far wider. It can be argued that Habitat itself has played a considerable part in making people more aware of design. In recent years, Habitat has introduced categorized ranges into its shops. Basics is a range of cheap and essential furniture; First Home goes a step further with simple, inexpensive but well-styled goods; City is sophisticated and has an emphasis on 'high tech' looks; Country is more comfortable and homely, using natural materials and finishes.

Tony Maynard and his team have had to bring a developing and more far-reaching Habitat to the public. He is promoting the furniture very strongly, taking care with the display and presentation of furniture in the stores. Carpeted room sets and plinths are used to emphasize the potential of a range. Furniture staff are encouraged to rationalize the information which they can give the public about the furniture. There have been too many forms of information with merchandise lists, summary pages in the catalogues, description lists, and the tags on the furniture. Habitat need to be precise. In categorizing the furniture into separate ranges, they are able to put across a number of images, not just one as in the past. There have been mistakes in display: 'We once put cheap upholstery in a massive Parisian apartment for the catalogue,' says Tony Maynard. 'It had a huge marble fireplace and a wooden floor. The furniture looked completely out of place. We have to be careful not to put things together in the shops that were never intended to go together. Of course there are overlaps and things from different ranges can be used but this must be tightly controlled.'

Mail order was first used by Habitat to reach customers in areas where a store had not been opened and to build up customers in places where a store was planned. Once the stores had spread over the country, in the mid-1970s, however, mail order continued. There was a mail order boom in Britain and clearly a market for mail order furniture and goods in their own right. Habitat at this time perfected a method for packaging fragile goods. Mail order is promoted strongly; the various methods used include selling specific products off the page in magazines, through direct mailings and, of course, the catalogue. Tony Maynard and his team feel they still have a lot to learn about mail order. The main aim of the company is in retailing, but it is his job to ensure the mail order side is well represented and run efficiently, rather than allowed to be steam-rollered by the store side. Maynard sees the catalogue as a three-way selling tool. First and foremost it is a mail order catalogue; it also acts as a store guide; and it is a magazine explaining Habitat and offering information, articles and advice; useful for staff and customers alike. The balance between those three elements has to be carefully maintained.

The catalogue is by no means the whole story. It reaches only 850,000 people. Habitat must look beyond this core to the millions who, though responsive to Habitat, will never buy a catalogue. This task is approached using various methods of marketing, and two of these are particularly effective. The first is the issue of leaflets, inserted in major magazines and mailed out to selected mailing lists, and the second is what Habitat calls 'product advertising'.

The leaflets usually reach a target market of five million people. The Basics leaflet, selling Habitat value for money, goes out each Spring and there is also a Christmas leaflet. 'The media will argue that you will lose out on readership by using leaflet inserts,' says Maynard, 'but we have found that it is far better in some instances to get a hard-selling leaflet into people's hands where it will be separated from other advertising material and therefore be far more persuasive.'

'Product advertising' works in a different way and at various levels. Individual products are sold off-the-page and this gives a short-term benefit to stores and mail order alike. More importantly, it makes people aware that Habitat sells a wide choice of products such as the one shown in the advertisement. Habitat is aware that these advertising methods, whilst successful, may be superseded as the company grows. Television is looked at periodically 'but it's expensive and we've not yet found a cost effective formula, but we will,' says Maynard.

Elsewhere Habitat exploits joint promotional opportunities with other companies. Recent examples include a promotion with Fiat (supporting the launch of the Panda and including a Conran Associates, specially designed, Habitat Panda) and with Barratts, the building company. An in-store video experiment has also been attempted in several stores.

The marketing methods reflect a keen awareness of the need to find opportunities for creating new business for the company: selling more Habitat merchandise to an ever increasing number of people. However the policies are tempered with a determination to proceed only with those products which will provide a profitable return for Habitat.

Marketing policies are decided at regular meetings held at either Wallingford or the London offices. Conran attends with Chris Turner, chief executive; Tony Maynard, marketing director; John Stephenson, a director of Habitat Mothercare; Malcolm Riddell, deputy managing director of Habitat Mothercare Group Design; Peter Hope, stores director, Alison Richards, buying director; Gill Lingwood, head of public relations, and Ann Sayer, Conran's secretary. Maynard draws up the agenda of subjects to be discussed – each of them proposed by a specialist. Gill Lingwood proposes any business arising from public relations, Malcolm Riddell does the same for advertising and Tony Maynard for sales, and so on. Long-term marketing objectives are agreed years in advance but the rules and methods are not tightly fixed. 'Terence is keen on good marketing and he knows that one has to be ready to change the rules in order to achieve long term objectives,' says Tony Maynard. Conran usually amends only details after discussions at the marketing meetings. As one of his staff has put it: 'Terence used to make the machinery, now he is oiling it.'

A typical marketing meeting might run along the following lines:

Maurice Libby, head of display, who has been called in to present his proposals for the Christmas window displays, shows two schemes because he knows from experience that no matter how confident he is in a particular theme, there is likely to be some reason put forward which may lead to it not being accepted. Everyone will contribute to a discussion and then Conran will make up his mind, very quickly, saying perhaps, 'That one's too overpowering, ideal for Dickens and Jones, but not for our merchandise. But that's the one.' It could be icicles and stalactites made in paper cut-outs. Maurice then continues with a presentation of possible promotion displays to be used on the walls and windows of the stores in the coming months. The discussion may centre around whether different colours should be used for each of the statements, constantly referring back to the need to sell the particular product and the Habitat look. Conran will put forward positive suggestions and make his preferences clear.

The meeting then goes on to consider the next item, which may be leaflets, followed by the promotions schedule for the next year, advertising, the new video experiments and the colour selection for table lamps for the next autumn range: should they add green to the existing red, blue and yellow? A media review would consist of a clear account of last year's advertising and proposals for the next year. Some colour magazines may be dropped because of a lack of response to the advertisements placed in them.

Products will often be discussed in great detail, particularly if a new range has recently gone into the shops and has been under promotion. How many of each item are selling? Are the colours right? The percentage of mail order sales could be an important item on the agenda, and Conran may suggest that the catalogue needs to be brighter, 'more *charmante*'. If a sales campaign, for a new season's stock, is being outlined, each piece of merchandise will be discussed and views may be aired on the need to find replacement pottery for that lost when a good supplier went bankrupt.

Colleagues say Conran may go to some lengths to make a point at these meetings, perhaps using what they consider to be cunning tricks. The point is always an important one and is purposely put before the whole meeting so that it can be discussed and agreed with everyone together. On one occasion, Conran wanted to use his old Soup Kitchen menus in a new in-store restaurant. One of the staff strongly opposed the idea. When the meeting broke for lunch Conran produced a complete Soup Kitchen meal; he ladled out various delicious soups, and handed round Cheddar cheese and French bread, thoroughly enjoying himself. Someone who was there remembers: 'We were awash to the gills with soup,' and Conran won the day. The menu went into the King's Road store a few weeks later.

OPERATIONS

With such a range of departments and so complex a structure, Habitat Mothercare requires a vital and efficient management team to oversee the general workings and strategies of the group. The person who co-ordinates this awesome task is Chris Turner, chief executive of Habitat.

In the past, when the company was smaller, members of management would take on various responsibilities and have several roles. Since 1977, Chris Turner has created around him a management team with general responsibilities for the company operations. Each one of them is a specialist in a particular field – be it retailing, marketing, data processing, or one of the other key areas for the company. In this way he has one person concentrating on one thing, but able to discuss problems and present aims and progress reports to the whole team. In the last eight years this core of experts, who work from Wallingford, have built up a good rapport and understanding. There have been no changes in the management team in that time – no one has left.

At monthly meetings the Habitat directors, joined by some senior executives, oil the day-to-day workings of Habitat. This may involve reviewing the profit forecast, looking at the company's objectives and priorities over the next period, altering pay structures, discussing personnel policies and staff requirements, deciding how many trainees are needed, and considering the desirablity of a new computer.

PERSONNEL POLICIES

All staff of the company are trained, on and off the job, from the first day they arrive. It is an essential and basic element of Habitat to maintain a staff who know what they are doing, why they are doing it, how to do it properly and how to develop in their jobs. Conran began with a small, enthusiastic staff whom he could involve in all aspects of his business. They worked for him for various reasons but many of them stress that job satisfaction and sheer enjoyment played a large part. Today the company is far too large to maintain the original informal approach to training. It is now highly organized, but an important element remains the identification of Habitat and why it is different from other stores and other companies.

New staff, at all levels, are given induction training and shown a company-made video entitled: *Habitat is Different*. People from all levels and all areas of the company took part in making it, including Conran himself. It provides a general introduction to the merchandising policies and the structure of the group. The training department provide training programmes appropriate to all staff which are given not only when new staff join but also after transfers or promotions. These are backed-up by training manuals on everything from company history to operating the telex machine, effective communication to industrial relations.

The company has three training centres where courses are run covering a range of skills including time keeping and time management; coaching techniques; leadership skills; interviewing skills and so on. All staff are encouraged to attend them. On-the-job training is continuous and all staff over eighteen are offered further education courses.

The company has found, to its cost, that, particularly on the retailing side, recruiting managers is a high risk policy. The present aim is to promote store managers from within the ranks of the staff. As a result there are training courses for floor managers, who will progress through the company store structure for four or five years, doing every job to floor manager, then assistant manager, and finally, if they make the grade, to store manager. In other areas too, staff who show potential for management are given six-month training programmes during which time their skills are identified. A network of management trainee schemes now exists.

In addition, all store staff attend a weekly, half-hour, in-store training session and staff progress is constantly appraised. Some will be selected to take part in the management training schemes, others may be moved to areas where their talents can be put to better use. In 1984 there is a drive to ensure the staff are well-informed about the products they sell; video films are used and detailed information from the buyers. All such schemes are intended not only to make staff more efficient, but also more relaxed and confident on the job.

Top management have long had what has been described as 'a share of the action' at Habitat. In 1976, a share scheme was introduced for all employees. Paul Clarke, a director of the Habitat Employees Share Trust Ltd, wrote in 1983, in the house magazine: 'Many businesses founder because of what has become known as the "Us" and "Them" divide. "Us" as does the work and "Them" as reaps the rewards.' To overcome this divide and create an environment in which employees and employers worked together towards the same end, Conran introduced a profit linked share scheme, enabling employees to become shareholders in the company. Senior executives had taken part in a share incentive scheme since 1971, when the company was relatively small and wanted to attract good managers. Conran wanted to extend the scheme to other staff from as early as 1972 but found that tax and company laws made it extremely difficult for employees to benefit. Conran fought for his own scheme and by 1976 had won, and he is very proud to have been a pioneer in this.

The number of shares given to a member of staff depends on length of service and the salary level. Shares allocated are held in trust for three years and if the person leaves in that time, the shares are lost to them, but pass to the people who stay. The amount allocated to the scheme each year depends on the profits of the company they work for. Shares are allocated to those companies which have contributed to that year's profits. 'Those who have not, do not get shares,' says Ian Peacock. 'We see which companies have contributed to group profits, then this company will be given an allocation of shares for the staff who have worked long enough to be eligible. This means they must have been employed continuously in that financial year in which the profits were made – usually at least eighteen months' service in the company is involved. Salaries are fixed quite independently of the share scheme and we aim to pay as well as anyone else in the retail business.'

PROPERTY

Starting out in London's Fulham Road before it became fashionable and breaking into New York via one of its least prosperous districts, Conran has long been acknowledged for his ability to find good sites, suitable premises and up-and-coming areas in which to situate his stores. And always at a favourable rent. Conran could not afford sites on High Streets in his early days, since he could not compete with normal rents. As ever, he turned a disadvantage into a bonus. Habitat stores made otherwise unpromising streets a focus for shoppers and as the chain expanded, so the company's bargaining power for obtaining the sites it wanted increased. Habitat had three important considerations in its favour: the successful conversion of supposedly marginal and impractical sites or buildings; its reputation for tough bargaining and achieving low rents; and its policy of maintaining local architectural styles when converting buildings. This is nowhere better shown than in the Canterbury store, which is a basic retail warehouse with flintwork matching the ancient buildings around it but which manages to combine with this a prominent display of the Habitat logo on the roof – three dimensional and created in steel – without debasing the general feel of the area. The day the store was opened the staff clambered onto the roof beside the grand logo and waved to their founder as his train passed by, directly behind the store.

In Plymouth Habitat is housed in one of the few remaining buildings which pre-date the last war – stylishly converted and situated in the midst of a sizeable car park and away from the main shopping centre. In Leeds the shop has no front in the traditional sense but instead an escalator sweeps customers inside what is otherwise a rather ordinary building.

Once a site has been found and negotiations are completed, the store management team get together with the people in Habitat Mothercare Group Design responsible for shop development. The store is then planned to the most minute detail, right down to fixtures and fittings. When a plan for building conversion and lay-out of departments has been agreed, the design unit work out a budget and draw up two specifications for the work required – one for building work and one for fixtures and fittings. Chris Turner then steps in to organize the opening of tenders. Which firms get the contracts for carrying out the work is decided by the management team of the whole group, the local store management and the designers. Usually the designer responsible will oversee the conversion once the contractor has been commissioned but occasionally, when the building is particularly complex as in Tunbridge Wells where a nineteenth-century church was used, an outside, specialist consultant is brought in.

Conversions for Habitat usually take three to four months and half-way through this work one of the management team will attend weekly on-site meetings 'to ensure we are getting the quality of work we are paying for'.

Meanwhile, staff are recruited locally and an experienced management team prepare to open. When the store is ready the designer hands over to the local area manager who by now has trained staff and organized stock into the nearest warehouse and is ready to move in. By opening day, the latest Habitat range will be displayed and the staff prepared to sell it to their new customers. This is achieved in about twenty-three days with the staff actually moving in to the premises and starting work three weeks before the opening, in order to prepare themselves and the shop. The first week is usually dedicated to staff training. By the second week the stock is arriving and the staff are placing it on the shelves which have been clearly marked to show which items go where. In the final week, when everyone is beavering away, top display people are brought in from other established stores who will inject their experience under the guidance of the store's display manager. Then the furniture displays go in and the final touches are made to give the new store a magnificent appearance for its opening. Maurice Libby, company display manager, says that 'entering an empty store is an exciting moment: this is the high spot – imagining how it will be'.

Meanwhile, the auditing and filing systems have been worked out and the store systems established – stock records, accounts, and the computerized check-out tills. The tills are tested and connected to the central computer at Wallingford.

Despite twenty years of Habitat and a highly motivated and experienced design team, there are no absolute rules. Expertise in judging how to lay-out and organize the display of stores has built up over the years and it could be imagined that there is now a tried and tested instant formula; yet this is not so. Each store is approached with a fresh eye and the lay-out and fittings created to best exploit that particular building, while always maintaining the Habitat atmosphere.

Maurice Libby explains: 'The aim is to bring the store alive, by the juxtaposition of various elements. In doing so we break most of the formal rules and our display staff are delighted to be given the freedom which this entails. Many of them come from other department stores and are technically trained so they are not intimidated when given responsibility for fifteen room sets and displays. Formally trained, mostly fashion oriented and often having found themselves restricted by the traditional rules of display, many of them come to us feeling bored with the lack of opportunity for self expression they have found in their work.

There are constant and insurmountable problems. Over the years endless types of shelving have been tried and tested – wooden shelves were tried and failed; the staining of shelves in blue was attempted in one store and some came out brightly while others hardly showed the colour. Air conditioning is another headache. Conran once suggested opening the doors of a store on the ground floor and the windows on upper levels to create a through draft rather than going to the expense of air conditioning. 'Forget it, with all those spotlights,' he was told. Lighting can create intolerable heat which makes both working and shopping under them unbearable. At one store, dozens of electric fans were brought in to counteract the effects of a heatwave. Colour schemes are enormously important, and not just for the walls and ceilings, but for handrails and other fittings. Habitat customers have come to expect something different and exciting when they enter a store. Again, there are no hard and fast rules and colours are decided depending on the look of the store – its shape and size. Some are old warehouses or even churches, some are traditional shop buildings. Natural lighting can vary from a broad expanse of windows to practically none at all.

With technological advances going ahead in leaps and bounds, the types of materials used are also highly flexible and open to new experiments and interpretations. 'For a long time we used dark-brown quarry tiles on the floors, but then looked at buff tiles and even coconut matting and sisal. Everything is tried out in the stores in the continuing quest for improved materials, more efficient systems, better lighting, air conditioning and so on – it never ceases.'

SYSTEMS

The central computers allow for price changes to be passed out to all stores immediately; for stock control to be constantly accurate and up-to-date; and for buyers to maintain a clear picture of what products are selling and where.

Each till in a Habitat shop is also a micro-computer which relays information to a central computer in order to keep a constant check on stock control, sales and takings. Such advanced systems are just beginning to be used in Britain today but Habitat have been using them since 1977. There were problems when the electronic tills were first introduced – they could store information on only 2000 products while Habitat stocked 6000. The system has been constantly updated since it was first installed, for in those eight years micro-computer technology has forged ahead.

8 The Catalogue

THE Habitat catalogue is a key instrument in the retailing scheme. Six per cent of total sales are through mail order, and the catalogue helps to promote sales throughout the year in all the stores.

Conran produced the first catalogue in 1966, using line drawings, printed on coloured sheets of paper, and fixed together through one corner. The results were not good, it was poorly organized and there was not enough stock to back it up. Then in 1969, at the time of the Ryman Conran merger, he produced another. The firm had just taken over Lupton Morton's furniture factory and warehouse in Wallingford where Tom Lupton and John Morton had been producing a catalogue called *Creative Living* for their wooden furniture. The new Habitat By Post catalogue was different in size and look; it incorporated, at the last minute, eight pages of Lupton Morton furniture, which had been re-photographed in the Habitat style. This included a range called Campus.

Guy Fortescue was working at Lupton Morton Design Studio at the time, above the British Crafts Centre in Earlham Street, having been taken on by them as a graphic designer straight from college to cope with the increasing number of catalogues and leaflets they were producing. He had been there six months or so when the works manager came in one day and started 'rushing from bank to bank transferring overdrafts in an attempt to keep at bay the suppliers' debt collectors who were sitting outside waiting for payments'. When they heard that Conran had taken over they were all anxious. Oliver Gregory, then head of the Conran Design Group, told Fortescue, 'We want you at Hanway Place at 9 am sharp tomorrow'. Guy, full of trepidation, was put to work on the catalogue. 'I asked if I could have some time to sort things out and he said, "Yes, you've got the rest of the afternoon."' About a year later, work started on the next catalogue. The small items were photographed in Conran's house in Regent's Park over one weekend. Zimmie Sasson was responsible for getting the items together and Conran and Guy Fortescue art-directed. The furniture was photographed in a barn at Conran's cottage at Dalham in Suffolk. 'We all stayed in various rooms in the cottage,' says Guy Fortescue. 'Terence and I shared the living room as far as I remember. He used to disappear at about six in the afternoon and let the rest of us get on with it while he prepared the evening meal, gigot or whatever.'

Roger Gain, a renowned French photographer, and a friend of Conran's, came over to do the photography, but was not used to the sort of pressure and pace which Terence demanded. The team were there for about three weeks, working extremely hard and living really well. 'That doesn't happen any more. It's one of the disadvantages of growing bigger,' says Fortescue, who is now responsible for the team of twelve permanent art directors, photographers and back-up people who produce the catalogue.

In 1972, when the company moved to Neal Street, the adjoining building was used as a photographic studio and Stafford Cliff took over the art direction of the catalogue, as one of the Conran Associates team. He began to add more imaginative and experimental ideas. 'Because it was just Terence, David Phillips and I, we were able to try out lots of different approaches, some of which helped establish the creative excitement the catalogue became known for, and which made it a collectors' item.' Some experiments were less successful than others but they always gave the products priority and let the ideas stem from the merchandise, rather than dominate it. 'I remember one year we tried to photograph a whole house in one picture, all the rooms were built as a cutaway, in a row, and people were walking from one room to another.' Some of the more complex compositions involved the photographer lying on precarious scaffolding arrangements and balancing his camera in one hand while shouting out which way to move a plate or arrange a chair, and clinging on for dear life with the other hand.

In 1974 they took studio space across the road in the large old warehouses of Earlham Street. The space was perfect – pine floors and tall ceilings – but with only a narrow lift to the second floor, all the sofas and storage units had to be winched up the outside of the building, swinging back and forth over the traffic.

For a couple of years Stafford Cliff designed and art directed the catalogues and Guy Fortescue concentrated on the graphics side, but as the pages increased Guy and Stafford shared the workload between them and began to build up a team of trainees. By this time, they had created a sort of rule book of things that worked and things that did not and things never to do again. 'It amuses me to look over other catalogues even now, and see how many traps we fell into – type over a textured or complicated background was always a favourite and always impossible to read.'

When Terence bought a house at Kintbury in 1973, they seized the opportunity to use the rooms as 'locations', before they had been furnished. Then the first French stores opened and houses in Paris and the French countryside were used as locations. The mixture of studio settings and real rooms gave the catalogue a reality which is still retained and developed today, making it a useful magazine full of home furnishing ideas. It gave the products freshness and impact that could not be achieved in store displays.

The catalogue became not only a selling tool but a guide to decorating the home and a statement about lifestyle. 'We often get customers who like one of the roomsets, and set out to copy every bit of it, then they write in to find out where even the plant in the pot came from. One year an antique shop, from whom we'd borrowed an old pine cupboard, got over two hundred requests for it, some people wanting it slightly taller, and some slightly narrower.' Today the use of non-Habitat props is kept to a minimum.

In 1977 the photographic studio was moved to the huge warehouse at Wallingford where the merchandise was all conveniently to hand. This involved photographers and art directors travelling down on Monday morning and staying in a local hotel all week, coming back (as they did, all in an old van, one year) on Friday nights. If they wanted a special flower for one shot, it had to be bought or picked on Monday and kept in the refrigerator, or rushed to them by train in the case of an emergency.

In those days the compiling of the catalogue was still rather happy-go-lucky but today it is assessed very carefully. Tony Maynard (marketing director, Habitat UK) now controls it. He sends a questionnaire to all store managers, key staff, and other people involved in the business, asking them to comment on all aspects of the catalogue. When the answers are returned he then evaluates the information and writes his creative brief, taking into account sales targets and print and production costs. In 1977 the catalogue was sold through newsagents for the first time.

'We talk to newsagents and discuss how to strengthen the distribution too, and I add my own personal opinions. With all this feedback we launch our plan: how much we should advertise, what form the advertising should take, how to promote the catalogue in the stores, what PR support it should have. The launch of the catalogue is very important to us because it gets a lot of press coverage and publicity generally.' Tony

Maynard has achieved a much wider audience and made many innovations including radio coverage and leaflets, constantly finding ways of expanding the Habitat appeal and ensuring people receive the message. It is now difficult finding new ways of improving the catalogue. The evaluation meeting, which is attended by Guy Fortescue, goes through every spread of the catalogue page by page and all comments from the group marketing committee are noted. 'What Terence has to say is taken very seriously but the consensus of opinion carries most weight. This meeting with the marketing committee is a springboard for creating the next catalogue and for deciding how new merchandise should be developing.'

Publication is in August. By the end of the previous November the designers get a list of all the merchandise the buyers think should go into the following year's catalogue. This means they have only three months' sales to go on when making decisions about the next catalogue. Of course, changes can be made at a late stage, but they are very expensive.

One of the things which has set the Habitat catalogue apart from others is the autonomy the designers have, though, of course, they must work to the buyers' brief. 'The majority of our design proposals are accepted but we always expect to adjust a few,' says Guy Fortescue. 'Often buyers feel some products should have more exposure than others and that can make the balance wrong visually. But for the most part the layouts sail through. The buyers and the marketing team supply the merchandise and sometimes give guidance to its presentation and selling points. If a product fails or succeeds, we have to decide how much it was to do with the merchandise itself and how much it was due to the way it was presented on the page. Of course we are influenced: an American store called Crate and Barrel have always had extremely good catalogues and in the early days a Swedish magazine called *Femina* contained some wonderful ideas. We look at French magazines such as *Maison de Marie Claire* and the German magazine *Schöner Wohnen*, but a lot of the influence is subliminal and we often pick up ideas from areas totally unrelated to Habitat. We never set out to copy others and the result is a catalogue which has created a look and reputation in its own right, doing a particular job and with a character of its own.'

The studios were set up at the industrial estate at Avonmore Road, near Olympia, where Habitat took over a building in 1977. They comprise some 10,000 square feet of space on two floors. The first contains a large photographic area capable of accommodating four or five room sets – kitchens, model rooms, props and set-building facilities. The ground floor is devoted entirely to warehousing all the furniture, kitchenware, fabrics, wallpapers, lighting, and accessories needed for each catalogue – it's the equivalent of a Habitat store. David Brittain, one of Europe's best known still life and roomset photographers, is on the staff and produces a large part of the work.

One photographer is not capable of producing all the pictures needed for the catalogue during the four months of shooting between February and May, so there is an ever changing rotation of freelance photographers, selected for their experience in each different area. 'We are a tremendous training ground for photographers,' says Guy Fortescue. 'They work very intensively for periods and quite a few started as assistants to previous photographers on the catalogue. When they break away to work for themselves they invariably come back to work for us until they move on and then perhaps we use *their* assistants. Rupert Watts for instance was the van driver and general dogsbody for the catalogue in Suffolk. His interest in photography grew to the point where he pestered one photographer to take him on as his assistant. Having gained even more experience as a result, he is now one of the catalogue's regular photographers and owns all his own equipment and has an assistant of his own.

'We also have set-builders, people to go out and get flowers and accessories, others to assemble and manœuvre furniture, we call them humpers, and someone to iron linens, make up curtains and generally prepare everything for each shot. It's a very intensive four months considering that a different catalogue for Habitat in France and Belgium is being prepared simultaneously. During the rest of the year there are other leaflets and "mailers" to produce but nothing is quite so hectic as those four months of catalogue production. The catalogue always comes out in August much to my wife's annoyance. I hate it for keeping me away from the garden in the summer. In the intensive months before its publication I sleep only four to five hours a night. I'm working from 5 am until 7.30 pm in the office and spend the whole evening checking copy when I get home. The kids suffer because when I am at home I relax by working in the garden and don't spend the time with them. You have to shut off from everything else to do the catalogue.' When it's published he goes on holiday for 'a bit of a breather' before the whole process starts again in September.

The earlier catalogues, he feels, were great to look through but some pages didn't sell the merchandise as well as they might have. There is a risk now, perhaps, that by concentrating too much on getting sales, it will become a little repetitive, so they keep adding new ideas and trying new techniques while still making it a selling catalogue. The Habitat catalogue has received awards in its own right and is in *Design and Art Direction*, the annual bumper volume of good graphics, regularly. Roy Strong, director of the V&A insists that it goes into the museum's archives every year. In the early days it was written entirely by David Phillips and his secretary Caroline Shaw. Then, as the catalogue grew, they started employing freelance writers. It is a challenging task to find writers creative in style and yet straightforward enough to bother with the code numbers and the price and size details, which are so important. Alexandra Towle, who later left to go to the publishing company Mitchell Beazley, developed some of the Habitat writing style – basically straightforward with some nice plays on words. 'I've had people who can write the mundane stuff but who don't have the creative flair, and I've had copywriters from advertising firms who can't be bothered with the huge amount of detail and just want to write headlines. In many respects the writing is the most difficult part of the whole catalogue,' says Guy Fortescue.

Like everything else the catalogue looks for Conran's approval. There is always the agonizing time after it has been delivered, while the team waits for everyone's reaction. Every transparency is carefully scrutinized down to the smallest details. 'One year we rushed the first copy through so that Terence had the first sight of it while he was sitting in the departure lounge on his way to America. He phoned his secretary and said, "Wonderful, we must have a party when I get back." '

9 The Boilerhouse

THE Boilerhouse Project, which opened in 1981, was a personal contribution to the design world by Conran himself. It was the first venture of a charitable organization, the Conran Foundation, and took the form of a museum and exhibition gallery housed in the V&A and intended to raise the level of discussion about design in this country and to provide stimulus for students, designers and for the manufacturing industry. Its first director is Stephen Bayley.

Conran had been a member of the Design Council from early on. When Sir Paul (later Lord) Reilly was the director, he invited Conran to chair one of the committees for the Design Council Awards, 'to liven them up when they were getting a bit staid,' says Reilly. On his retirement as director of the Design Council, Lord Reilly accepted an invitation to become a director of Conran Associates and the two men maintained their close contact. The idea for the Boilerhouse had been mooted in 1978 when Conran had had a chat with Lord Reilly. Conran explained that he wanted, with his own money, to start a collection of modern design to inspire students and young designers. Reilly had met Stephen Bayley at a dinner party in 1976 and had commissioned a book by him, *In Good Shape*, which was published by the Design Council in 1979. 'Stephen had an idea much the same as Terence's and at that dinner he said he was looking for a rich man to sponsor it. So when Terence mentioned his idea to me it seemed sensible to put the two in touch with each other.' Conran and Bayley were invited to Lord Reilly's house in Kensington to discuss the project and found they got on very well.

Stephen Bayley, with a lively mind and an art history background, was well qualified for such a job. When he left school he had considered becoming an architect but 'didn't want to spend seven years learning how to do it', so he changed the course to art history which he felt 'was probably related to architecture'. He took a degree at Manchester and then an MA at Liverpool School of Architecture and taught at Liverpool College of Art and then at the Open University, at Milton Keynes. 'I learned so much there,' says Stephen. 'I was called a lecturer but I enjoyed the writing, producing, presenting which the Open University demanded, and really became a sort of TV broadcaster.' From there he joined the University of Kent as a lecturer and was set on establishing a serious academic career. 'I'd always been interested in Terence Conran, and when I edited the Jubilee edition of *Architectural Review* in 1977, I interviewed him for that issue – that was when I met him for the first time. About a year later I was in some elaborate seminar when I got a call from Paul Reilly who said "Come and meet Terence". I came up from Kent on my new folding bicycle, full of excitement. Terence was stomping around Reilly's drawing room with a twelve-inch cigar in his hand. "I've made a lot of money," he said. "I don't want to leave it all to the children or the Inland Revenue; I want a collection to inspire students and young designers." That was the word he used, "Collection".

'Having got used to the tedium and slowness of university it was very exciting and the energy of the thing attracted me. Terence gave me £1,500 to go round the world to make sure no one had already embarked on a similar enterprise.' Bayley travelled to New York and Washington, visiting several museums including the Museum of Modern Art and the Smithsonian; he went to museums in Oslo, Munich and Berlin and did indeed establish that although museums staged exhibitions on design, nobody was planning anything of the kind he had in mind. In 1979 he wrote 'my pompous report' with the intention of establishing the Conran Foundation, it was submitted to the Charity Commissions and the Foundation became a registered charity. Ever optimistic, Bayley confidently expected to leave the university the following week, but the funding for the project was to come out of the money gained by the flotation of Habitat as a public company. When the idea of the Conran Foundation was first being discussed in 1978 it was thought the flotation would take place in 1979. In the event it didn't happen until the end of 1981.

'I was stuck in Kent for another two years before the new museum opened. The original idea was that we were going to build something in Milton Keynes – wistful thought – with a project based on an idea something like the Sainsbury Centre at the University of East Anglia, near Norwich [where Norman Foster's great barnlike building is used to house the Sainsbury family's collection of art, and to have temporary exhibitions]. We had in mind a sort of high tech warehouse with stacker trucks taking interesting objects out of Dexion shelving to show students. In the meantime, another space became available. Terence was on the advisory board of the v&A Museum and Roy Strong, director of the museum, with characteristic initiative, offered a space within the building, conveniently situated in Kensington.'

The Boilerhouse space was chosen from two unattractive but potentially useable sites in the V&A; one called Clinch's Hole, in the middle of the museum, the other the old boilerhouse yard on the museum's western boundary, opposite the entrance to the Science Museum. Of the two, the old boilerhouse yard was chosen because it seemed to offer a potentially more efficient space for the first generation of activities of the Conran Foundation. At first the area, divided into many rooms, was not promising but then some daring demolition of partition walls revealed – without catastrophe – a large open space which has become one of the biggest exhibition halls devoted to design anywhere in Europe.

Stephen Bayley, introducing the project in the *International Journal of Museum Management and Curatorship* wrote: 'It is relatively unusual in modern Britain to have private enterprise investing in an institution with a public purpose, but the ideas which move the people concerned with The Conran Foundation can trace their origins to the beginning of the nineteenth century when a Parliamentary Committee published a Report on Arts and Manufacturers in 1836. Then as now, there was an awareness that British industry was failing and there was a similar anxiety about hostility towards imports which we feel today.' One hundred and fifty years ago, he pointed out, British manufacturers were concerned about the French ribbon and lace pouring into Britain. Now we are more alarmed by German cars and Japanese electronics, but the problem is the same. Other countries are producing better designs and the British want to buy their products rather than home-grown goods.

The Boilerhouse is concerned with all aspects of mass-produced material culture, in other words, design. There are a fair number of museums which hold exhibitions concerned with design – graphics, textiles, product design – throughout the world, including New York's Museum of Modern Art and others in Germany and Scandinavia, and they have helped to develop modern industrial design. They have also managed to interest the public in a subject which is not taken seriously enough by the art establishment in Britain.

Bayley felt that exhibitions in the late seventies tended to rely on craft-based design rather than design for manufacturer, when design became a subject for an exhibition. Manufacturers, designers and the general public were starved of example and stimulation. Bayley felt he should follow the philosophy of Henry Cole, founder of the V&A, who

This picture appeared in the front of the 1971 Autumn and Christmas catalogue, which was put together about a year after the end of the Habitat/Ryman merger. Despite the setbacks, Habitat was well-established, offering the complete home range of furnishings and accessories, as this studio flat shows. The chairs and sofa come from the popular Scoop range; the tables are by Magestretti; on the platform is a Habitat divan bed, duvet and headboard; in addition the worktop for the desk and the four-drawer chest were from Habitat.

Magestretti chairs, shown here with a Larry, white laminate, table (*above*), are
typical of classic Habitat furniture – a solid beech frame and handwoven rush seat.
The Bauhaus chair is another longstanding Habitat favourite (*below left*) – simple
lines in an elegant design. The Cypress chair (*below right*) is a solid pine
construction with tough, woven-rush seating.

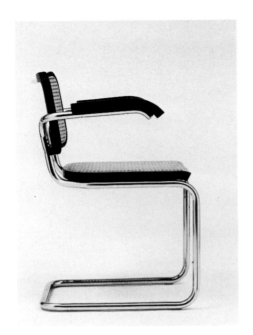

The Director's chair first appeared in the Habitat range in 1970 and has been a
bestseller ever since. Its attraction lies not only in its good looks and strong
construction but also its versatility as a folding chair and one that can be used
indoors or out.

Conran sold the classic Chesterfield sofa before he opened his first Habitat shop. It was then produced by Phillip Pollock's Aerofoam company, from a design sketched by Conran on the back of an envelope. Today it continues to sell in large numbers. It is shown here with two Wassily chairs in black leather, another superb design, created by Marcel Breuer in 1926 and named after Wassily Kandinsky, his fellow student at Germany's Bauhaus Institute.

Two of the luxury ranges of upholstered furniture produced for Habitat over the years were Country House, with the ample four-seater sofa shown here (*below*), and William, a simple, stylish and comfortable design (*above*).

An eye-catching Christmas window will attract customers (*above left*) and a special promotion, such as Kitchen Market in 1984 (*above right*), creates a focus for Habitat's wide range of cookery and tableware. The catalogue not only promotes goods but can itself be imaginatively promoted, as seen in this advertisement (*below*).

Barney Goodman worked with Selim Zilkha through
the founding and development of Mothercare. He
continues as its chairman since the merger with
Habitat, an important indication of the ease and
optimism which surrounded the coming together of
the two large retailing organizations.

Sir Terence Conran, chairman of the Habitat
Mothercare group, which now includes Habitat,
Mothercare, Heal's, NOW and Richard Shops;
Conran Associates; an advertising company;
publishing company; contract furniture business; the
Neal Street Restaurant; and other projects.

Stafford Cliff, a highly-respected designer, started as
an office junior for the Conran Design Group in
1968. He is now creative director of Conran
Associates.

Priscilla Carluccio is a director of Habitat
Mothercare. She first became involved with Habitat
in France and later ran The Conran Shop.

Terence Conran designed this interior (*top*) as a feature for the 1981/2 catalogue using that year's range of Habitat furnishings, accessories and fabrics.

This magnificent pine four-poster bed (*left*) was created for Habitat in 1981 and is shown here with a matching pine-veneered blanket box and other Habitat accessories.

The delightful 'Catherine Wheel' fabric covering the nostalgic Zozo sofa was featured as a border for the front of the 1976 catalogue and was available as fabric and wallpaper.

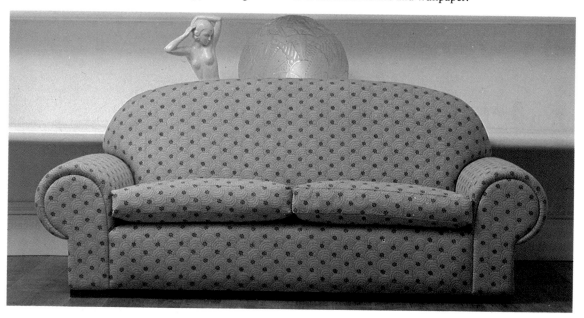

In the early 1960s Conran's home on Regents Park Terrace (*opposite below*) reflected his love of good design and simple interiors. His present home, Barton Court, was a base for work in 1978 (*opposite above*) when he had an office constructed there. The main living room (*opposite centre*) contains a carefully chosen mixture of antiques, personal treasures and modern designs. The main bedroom (*above*) is stark and empty. The beautiful gardens can be glimpsed from the hallway (*overleaf*).

wanted his museum to be 'specially commercial in so commercial an age' and 'an abrasive stimulus to the public and at the same time a service to industry and business'.

Bayley's first task was to put on a challenging series of exhibitions about the history, theory, process and practice of design. The first year saw five exhibitions; 'Art and Industry: A Century of Design in the Products You Use', was the first. It set out to show how fine art had influenced product design. 'The conventional art-historical assumption is that one of the chief cultural phenomena of the twentieth century is the influence of industry on art. By reversing that statement it can be seen how artists have in fact influenced the products of industry.' In some cases a particular designer's work was looked at in detail; there were comparisons between the products of particular manufacturers then and now: an old Bissell carpet sweeper for instance next to the modern version.

The following exhibition was a calculated contrast, concerning the past, present and future of Sony, the Japanese consumer electronics manufacturer. It included a historical survey of key products, with critical comments, and a survey of production, showing some hitherto secret future products, and an analysis of how the design fits into Japanese industrial management. The Sony exhibition was followed by a travelling exhibition of the work of the German designer Dieter Rams, with examples of his many designs for Braun and also of his furniture designs. The exhibition was designed by Rams himself who felt the pure white shell of the Boilerhouse was ideal for showing off his slick, sophisticated and mainly black products.

'52 Months to Job One; How they Designed the Ford Sierra' came next and coincided with the launching of Ford's new model to replace the Cortina. The year ended with an exhibition called 'Memphis: Milano in London', a presentation of avant-garde furniture, glass, ceramics and fabric design from the Italian Memphis group, inspired by Ettore Sotsass.

The Boilerhouse came in for much criticism in its first year, received an enormous amount of publicity and fulfilled its aim of being abrasive. The newspapers reacted with a curious, though characteristic suspicion of anything tainted with the word 'design'. *The Guardian* felt that an exhibition about everyday consumer goods, who designed them and why, 'might have been calculated to distance the public', while *The Observer* declared, with some consternation, that 'the work of the industrial designer would be sinister if it were not also mildly ridiculous.... The Boilerhouse is a strange nether-region where the homage paid to goods and gods is wreathed around with dubious assumptions.' On the other hand, radio found things to admire and *The Financial Times* commented that 'Terence Conran's new Boilerhouse gallery of industrial design continues to carry a startling message.'

In its second year the Boilerhouse brought in an exhibition of Danish design packaged by the Danish Design Centre, a neat and faultless display of goods designed and made in Denmark over the past fifty years. The story of the product development was illustrated in each case by drawings, photographics and schematic diagrams. The exhibition, which was conceived with a showing at the Boilerhouse in mind, had travelled from Denmark via New York, Chicago, and Los Angeles, and then went on its way round Europe.

A retrospective view of the work of Kenneth Grange came next. He is one of Britain's best-known product designers, belonging to a generation of writers, fashion designers, painters and film makers who created the distinctive flavour of Britain in the sixties. This was a highly personal account of one man's philosophies and working techniques, his successes and even some of his failures, and the delight of the exhibition was that the products were so familiar to the public: the Kodak instant camera, Wilkinson Sword razors, parking meters, sewing machines, hair dryers and other everyday objects.

'Images for Sale' was an exhibition about the design elements which service Britain's advertising business and this was followed by the most controversial exhibition yet, called 'Taste', which caused critics to scoff. Many thought it did not work entirely; the products shown were themselves fascinating and attracted students, who were to be seen sketching throughout the duration of the exhibition and in that respect the Boilerhouse was certainly doing the job intended. Some say it was 'far and away the most successful exhibition in London and the most widely reported design event since The Festival of Britain'.

The end of 1983 saw a small but entertaining exhibition of the quirky sculptures of Philip Garner, with Garner himself creating some exhibits in front of the public. The first exhibition in 1984 took a more serious look at the design of modern hand tools.

Design being so various a subject – employing art, materials, science and commerce – that no one Boilerhouse exhibition was ever intended to be complete in itself. Instead the programme of exhibitions is meant to have a cumulative effect so during the Foundation's five-year tenure of its museum space, the public is given a wide view of the different components in the culture of the everyday.

Before the Foundation moves into its own permanent premises at the end of 1986, the Boilerhouse will continue to put on exhibitions – about robots, trucks, failures, fashions and disposables – which extend, and even bend, the borders of the exhibition concept. Incidentally, by being provocative and popular they also bring a new public into the V&A.

The Boilerhouse tries to make design an everyday reality. The educational idea is to make the visitors read objects like they read books, so that as consumers they can be more discerning and more articulate in their condemnation of sham and ugly products. When this happens retailers and manufacturers will be forced into higher standards. In a way, the idea is the same as Habitat.

10 Mothercare

A FEW months after Habitat became a public company in Autumn 1981, it merged with Mothercare. The Mothercare merger had very little in common with the earlier Ryman fiasco. There was none of the haste and panic, none of the animosities and recriminations that had beset the earlier marriage. Terence Conran had admired both the Mothercare business and its owner, Selim Zilkha. Ever since his youth he had been attracted by success and strong personalities. On his side Selim Zilkha had chosen Terence specifically as the person he would like to take over his stores. Mothercare was a chain of 423 stores selling clothes and equipment for pregnant women and small children, operating in ten countries, much larger than Habitat, and a highly efficient business.

Habitat and Mothercare both started at much the same time, in the early sixties. Selim Zilkha, from a banking family, was young, energetic and very rich. He had become bored with banking and tried one or two other things as an alternative. His interest in shops for the mother-to-be-and-her-baby was first aroused shortly after the war when he came across the Prenatal shops in France. He could see this market in the UK was not being adequately catered for. Expectant parents had to go to several different shops to get the things they needed and he felt this was a bad deal for the consumer. There were other bad deals too: would-be parents always had to put down a deposit on any goods they ordered and then if something awful happened, a miscarriage, for instance, they couldn't get their money back.

Selim Zilkha had bought, with other investors, a chain of about ten chemists shops called Lewis and Burrows. One of the shops was a large branch at Kingston-upon-Thames, South London. Zilkha decided to try a mother-to-be-and-baby department in the Kingston branch. He knew nothing about the business but he acquired a buyer or two and put the merchandise on the first floor where a colleague described it as a complete fiasco. After two years the new operation was some £180,000 in the red, so in 1960 he sold that business and bought a chain of old-fashioned pram and nursery furniture shops called W. J. Harris. There were fifty shops in London and the home counties with large, old-fashioned letter-ing over the door and long, narrow interiors full of prams and sewing machines. He sold off twenty-five of these shops and with the other twenty-five he started his nursery furniture business and changed the name to Mothercare.

M. Mazard, the managing director of Prenatal, the original model for his idea, was taken on as adviser for the mother-to-be-and-baby business in England. Zilkha added the maternity wear and layette to the prams and cots but again did very, very badly. Although he was paying M. Mazard a fee for being allowed to study exactly the methods of the French shops and though he was modelling his chain on them it still wasn't working in Britain.

In 1963, Zilkha met Barney Goodman, an astute and able businessman who had been working with Joe Hyman at the hugely successful textile company, Viyella, since the fifties. 'I told him I was thinking of starting a business in competition,' says Goodman. 'Zilkha said "I am very happy to talk to you and tell you everything I can". Selim is a very nice man. We were together for five hours discussing the business and we got on well. The following day we chatted again and eventually he said "Don't start on your own business, come in with me." Although I knew nothing about retail I went in with him in 1963 and we became very great friends. We thought we would like to be the Marks & Spencer of the mother-to-be-and-baby business.'

Zilkha and Goodman decided the most important priorities were to learn about distribution of stock and to have good people working for them. They divided the business fairly evenly between them: Zilkha looking after systems and finance and doing the hardware buying and Goodman covering personnel and software buying. They divided the property buying between them. 'We were taking quite small shops and we improved the merchandise, the people and the systems. We got ourselves well known by advertising and we built the business over twenty years. Selim was a great virtuoso.'

In 1967 Zilkha was talking about going into the European Free Trade Area. Mothercare is among the very few British firms who have had the courage to go into Europe and the determination to make the venture work. Both Habitat and Laura Ashley were to follow their example. They went into Denmark first, opening a store in March 1968, followed in November by the first Swiss store. In 1969 they opened a store in Zurich and one in Stockholm and started the mail order business in Norway. In 1970 they went into Germany and Austria, and in 1975 into Holland and in 1977 into Belgium.

Way ahead of their time, Mothercare had introduced a computer system which was to make them a highly efficient operation as early as 1964. They invested in the computer before they really needed it, while they were still expanding, so that they could learn how to use it. It cost much more than they could afford at the time but they saw that it would speed up and streamline the retailing to such an extent that in a short time it would pay for itself. They were right. Partly because of their computer and partly because of their excellent training scheme, they became, and probably still are, the most efficient retailing venture in the world. Everything was computerized: labels, print out, catalogue, stock. The computer indicates how much each store has sold, twice a week. It has inbuilt information on seasonal merchandise. Originally monitored once a week, it is now programmed to take a half-yearly and yearly view of sales and can predict with the utmost precision what merchandise each store will need at any period of the year.

Shortly after they had installed the computer, the BBC made a television programme about Mothercare, called 'Blueprint for Growth' in which Zilkha and Goodman explained where they thought they were going, laying down their philosophy of the business and their explanation of its success. The film is in black and white and has odd hitches and quirks which would never be allowed on a modern film, but it is fascinating. It opens unashamedly with a heart-warming glimpse of a sleeping baby and the sound of a cash register. BBC Radio's Brian Redhead introduces Selim Zilkha who speaks earnestly, and Barney Goodman, who talks with conviction about their aims and their belief in the need for a proper 'systems-based' business. The film shows quite clearly how they would manage to run an international retailing business with outlets in Scandinavia, Europe, the UK and America from a central computer in Watford. All the ordering for all the stores in the UK and Europe is still done from Watford and the manufacturers send the goods direct to the individual stores.

Rosemary Good (now marketing director) joined the firm as public relations officer in 1967. 'Selim was like Terence,' says Rosemary Good, 'he was always there. He used to work seven days a week from 7.30 am – he was the idol of efficiency.'

On 15 July 1976 Mothercare bought a chain of retail shops in the United States. They had problems at first, as all the British have found in the USA, and in the end they did not try to make the American shops the precise equivalents of those in Europe. They are smaller and concentrate

110

more on clothes and fashion. In the UK only about seven per cent of the merchandise sold is maternity wear, in America it is more like forty per cent; the clothes in America were always high fashion whereas in the UK they tended to look more drab. In 1976 Barney Goodman moved across to America to run the business over there.

The key to the marketing techniques of Mothercare has been the catalogue, revised at the end of every July and January to hit the spring and autumn buying periods. It is designed to allow the housebound expectant family to work out its investment before entering the store and its effects were noticed from the moment it first appeared. Not only did it allow those British towns without stores to benefit from Mothercare products but orders began to arrive unsolicited from all over the world.

After twenty-two years of successful expansion and trading, why did Selim sell out? Boots and Littlewoods and Woolworth had come in to the cheap end of the baby market and instead of moving upmarket Mothercare had tried to compete with them. In the latter years of Zilkha's reign, the clothes merchandise became a bit dull. Mothercare ignored the wish of the public for brighter colours and were nervous of the competition. They decided to go down in price with their competitors and that was their big mistake. 'Boots used to wait for our catalogue to be published and sell similar objects 5p cheaper,' says Kevyn Jones, Managing Director of Mothercare.

When Mothercare sales started to drop in 1980 or so, Zilkha felt he had been in the business long enough. He was a young and rich man when he started the business in 1961 and didn't need to keep it on. 'He liked to think of changing his life every twenty years,' says Barney Goodman. For any deal that Zilkha made, Goodman's support was crucial. And they did not just go to the highest bidder. Only the one firm caught their fancy: Habitat. Both men admired its style, its success and its chairman and founder, Terence Conran.

Goodman explains, 'We went to Terence because we thought he could add to the business what it lacked and we didn't ourselves understand. I'd known Terence for fifteen years and always thought he was a tremendous goer.' When the takeover was first announced everyone at Mothercare was dismayed, but Barney Goodman remained in England for a period as a smoothing and confidence-inspiring influence and things soon settled down.

'It was quite a struggle for me,' he says, 'keeping everyone happy, dealing with new people. We were highly organized, very successful market leaders with the best systems and retail operation in the world. The merchandise did become a little hum drum for a year or two, but Terence got control of something very beautiful under unique circumstances.' Habitat Mothercare was formed in December 1981.

John Stephenson was switched from running Conran Design Associates to head the relaunch of Mothercare and immediately initiated a research programme which revealed that 'We were perceived as classless and with as good a visibility as M & S, but there were unwelcome perceptions too. Our clothes were thought of as dull and synthetic.

'We had to make changes that would keep our existing downmarket audience but at the same time add the Habitat type of customer. Mothercare were not making losses when we took over, but lower profits, certainly. There was competition, of course, from the traditional clothing retailers like Littlewoods and Marks and Spencer and on maternity clothes from department store chains like C & A, but no one else was presenting a complete package for mothers, expectant mothers and kids up to ten. Middle-class mothers were buying their good-value baby carriages with us but went elsewhere for their clothes. Mothercare's maternity clothes were felt to be all right for slumming around the house with a broom and iron but missed the career woman interrupting her business life to have a baby and the stores were found to be a bit clinical (though interestingly this was very much liked by mothers in the baby part of the stores).'

Kevyn Jones, now managing director of Mothercare UK and Europe and a director of Mothercare Stores Inc., joined the firm in 1969 and as a raw Welsh recruit remembers helping to open the Llandudno branch where 'there must have been six Joneses in the shop who all used to want to speak Welsh to each other all the time'. Until 1980 Mothercare was doing very well and nobody in the city would have been saying that a change was needed. 'We always had a very good baby business but lacked the design input needed to improve the fashion side until Conran took over.'

What has surprised him is to discover that fashion 'really is a science', and that the designers seem to be able to take in colours and identify the ones that will be fashionable in a year's time. The buyers are seen to be vitally important in this process. New designs came from joint decisions between the buyers and the designers and the buyers have the final say in what is selected from completed designs. The intention was to develop the upmarket side of business which is what the shops lost over the previous few years. The design element, so vital to the rebirth of Mothercare, was very cautiously added.

Conran may have bought Mothercare thinking 'I can do a Habitat' but he soon realized there was an enormous turnover from 'lower common denominator' customers whom he must not upset. Nevertheless, the company had been going downhill and Conran felt it was because price had been the only criterion. 'If you cut out style you cut out the enjoyment in life. People cannot exist on value for money alone,' he says. Though Mothercare was still extraordinarily cheap, parents were beginning to say that wasn't enough and why weren't the clothes more interesting and fun. Mothercare had been keeping prices low by bullying their suppliers. They used to have an annual suppliers' conference, which has been described as 'worse than a crucifixion'. All innovation had stopped because all they were doing was keeping the supply lines open at the right price. The merchandise stagnated and so did the company.

The merchandise director, Marlene David, joined in 1964 and stayed with the company until 1983. She had previously trained as a nurse at Great Ormond Street Hospital. She had done a tremendous job over the years but 'has rather a strict sense of what's what' and found it difficult to change. The layout of the old stores was very costly too because each store had to look identical to the last detail. There was a manual for the plan which applied to each store and inevitably this became tedious and the customers became bored with it. The Mothercare team decided things had to be changed and saw several ideas in the US which they tried to put into practice in their own stores. 'We didn't do it well and we made lots of mistakes, but we were realizing that something needed to be done,' says Kevyn Jones. What Conran did was to introduce subtle changes so as not to throw the baby out with the bath water. 'It's like a packet of Swan Vestas matches, the changes are imperceptible but keep up to date', he says. 'We started by just listening and talking with the staff who produced many ideas. So the stores and merchandise did improve, but in no way to shock already loyal customers: mirrors here, pastels there, a carpet underfoot, softer lighting. The effect was pleasant but not startling.' Conran has gone about it in 'a very good way – a hands-off way. He hasn't rammed Habitat down people's throats, staff or customers.'

The *Daily Express* expressed it thus: 'From the moment Terence took over the company there was intense speculation about the meaning of the marriage and the future of the two component parts, both individually and together. This speculation was intensified by an eighteen month period of uncharacteristic circumspection for a group which traditionally revels in a high profile. Barely a squeak came out of the group, making it clear that the new bosses were not about to tinker with Mothercare for short term strategical reasons but would wait until the new Look could be launched with certainty and authority. On the first anniversary (actually eighteen months later) they launched the new catalogue with a more cheerful, brighter, more optimistic Mothercare.'

The launching of the new catalogue to the city and the press was a celebration of the first eighteen months work and the £19 million profit the two companies had made during the year following the merger. Terence Conran and Barney Goodman arrived on stage each propelling a pushchair.

There was a fashion show with small booths laid out in the manner of shops and the front stage was an enormous Mothercare store front. There were slides and a video show displaying the sweet-pea colour scheme for the shops. Habitat and Mothercare people were there in force and so were the press. 'The ranks of grey-suited stockbrokers attending the launch decided they liked the sweet peas too. Mothercare shares blossomed 12p to 284p,' said the *Daily Express*.

Sebastian Conran, Terence's eldest son, did much of the designing for the new Mothercare hardware products. And it wasn't just the press who were impressed at the launch. The Habitat and Mothercare people were themselves bowled over. Mothercare is efficient, the staff are wonderful, the training is excellent but the input from the Habitat side of the business is invaluable. 'I think everyone saw themselves for the first time, truly as part of one group', said Malcolm Riddell.

Terence was quick to point out that what the world saw was just a beginning. 'We are going to produce an improvement in function and physical appearance of the prams and pushchairs. He pointed to a page of photographs in a *Which?* article on pushchairs. "Look," he said, "you can see by only looking at that page what a lot of design work needs to be done." '

The launch presented new colours of pink, blue and green. The new children's wear had much more cotton, simpler designs, plainer but brighter colours. The maternity wear was much improved. There were pushchairs with reflector wheels ('Be seen – Be safe') and much more new merchandise which went with a whole new set of encouraging catchphrases, used in the catalogue and in the store display: 'Bags of Fun'; 'Wrap up Warm'. The new catalogue was wider and more generous looking and featured a booted, wind-tousled family walking through an English winter countryside. It could have been family Conran themselves, fifteen years back. It included a little article on breast feeding your new baby and a photograph of a girl with her head in a towel examining her still-slim pantie girdled hips in a white tiled bathroom with a white-painted bentwood coat hanger under the heading 'Basis for Comfort'.

Comparisons and links between Mothercare and Habitat are not readily drawn within the company. There is a very conscious effort to maintain the two as separate trading chains except for behind the scenes activities such as investment. Each has to reach its objectives quite separately though there are small links and cross references in the two mail order catalogues and in some fabric and wallpaper ranges. On the subject of fashion, John Stephenson repeats one of his familiar philosophies, 'the merchandise is the message', which means that you can spend all you like on shopfitting but it won't do much for your sales figures if the goods aren't right. Nonetheless, in the trial refit at Kilburn, even without the new merchandise, there was a sales increase of five to six per cent in the revamped store with no other form of promotion, so obviously the stores themselves are crucial as part of the packaging. The idea of course is to expand. Stephenson's thinking is to try to build larger, more manageable centres. So Mothercare is more likely to expand the West German chain before having a go in France. In 1983 there was a curious scattering of stores in Europe which included six in Austria, three in Belgium, three in Holland, three in West Germany, eleven in Switzerland and one each in Norway, Sweden and Denmark. In America the geographical spread is even more of a problem, the stores are scattered like confetti, but again they will be built into larger, geographical groups which can be more intensively managed. The remarkable result of the new look is that Mothercare still has no competitor on the horizon. 'If someone had been quick on their feet ten years ago, it would have been different,' says John Stephenson.

11 Heal's

JOHN Harris Heal went into the feather-dressing trade with a firm in Leicester Square and in 1810 started a feather-dressing business of his own. In 1818 he moved into a shop at 203 Tottenham Court Road, six doors down from the present site, where he became a mattress and feather bed manufacturer.

When he died his son, John Harris II, ran the business with his mother and in 1840 they bought up the premises known as Millers Stages at 196 Tottenham Court Road and built their bedding factory with a feather dressing mill, a stove machine for carding the wool and a steam plant for dressing and purifying the feathers.

This was the John Harris Heal who established the real fortunes of the firm, helped by a time of great national prosperity. He was one of the first retailers to see the benefits of advertising and he advertised in the monthly partworks of Dickens' stories for twenty-eight years, beginning with *Pickwick Papers* in 1837, following on in seven more novels and ending up with *Our Mutual Friend* in 1865. He also advertised in Thackeray's partworks. He consistently publicized his goosefeather beds, 'French Bedding' and eiderdown quilts in the *Illustrated London News*, in *Punch*, *The Spectator*, *The Times*, *Morning Post*, *Herald*, *Standard* and *Chronicle*. Not forgetting the ladies, he advertised in *Household Words*, *Family Herald*, *The Ladies' Newspaper* (later *Queen*), *London Society*, *Bell's Weekly*, and more. To reach other sections of the public he used *The Field*, *Art Journal*, *Notes and Queries* and Murray's *Handbook for Travellers on the Continent*. He also posted bills on station platforms.

When the Crimean War broke out, he produced an illustrated catalogue of 'Officers' Equipment for the War' showing tent bedsteads, portable furniture and other field equipment, with a picture of a horse loaded with 'Officers' Equipage for Campaigning as Invented and Used through the Peninsular War'. He continued to issue this army catalogue until 1855.

However, the mainstay of the business was, and always had been, the 'contriving and the making of beds of superlative comfort'. He made bedding in fine fleece or horsehair, white goose feathers, the purest down and stout linen bedticks: his beds were quite outstanding. He used to claim that his real eiderdown for bed quilts was far lighter than ordinary goose down and had the advantage of being warmer. He may have believed this himself but it doesn't seem to have been proved. In his early days the goosefeather bed was the backbone of the business and was used with a straw palliass on the four post bedstead until 1844 when spring mattresses were introduced.

He produced a hundred editions of his price-list between 1844 and 1874 and the earliest illustrated catalogue came out in 1852, largely devoted to mahogany four post and half tester bedsteads, though by that time the metal bedsteads were already fashionable: there are sixty-seven patterns of iron- and brass-canopied or low-headed bedsteads and children's cribs in this catalogue.

For the Great Exhibition in 1851 Heal & Son staged a particularly elegant set of bedroom furniture specially designed by J. Braune in the Louis XVI style. It was in mahogany, enamelled a soft shade of cream and with gilded enrichments carved in lime. The centre of attraction was the elaborate half-tester bedstead with embroidered hangings of pearl-white satin, lined with cerise coloured silk. The complete set would have been priced at least at £2,000, an exorbitant figure. An eiderdown quilt with an embroidered, crimson satin covering was shown at the same exhibition. The salesmanship and quality of the goods was very good at this stage but the design was almost nonexistent. Mock Gothic was in vogue for expensive furniture and for the most part the mouldings were coarse and ugly; chair backs were built up on iron frames bent into plain but graceless curves.

Heal's was then selling an expensive stuffed spring mattress which was cumbersome and awkward. John Harris devised a form of spring mattress at a reasonable price which was light and easily moved for cleaning. It was made in three parts, ingeniously hinged and lashed together with highly tempered steel springs enclosed in a specially woven stout linen cover made to his own specification. He patented it in 1860 under the fashionably French title *Sommier Elastique Portatif.* More than one hundred years later it is still being made.

John Harris was now supplying retailers with his beds and issued a special price-list for the trade. During the eighteen fifties and sixties the business expanded very rapidly, developing from the original feather dressing concern into an important furnishing house. The extended Tottenham Court Road frontage had taken on an imposing appearance, the fascia, embellished with decorated tiles, was supported on an arcaded shop front of cast iron. It was designed by architect J. Morant Lockyer, an authority on Italian Renaissance architecture. Of its day it was one of the larger London shops. At the back ran two long galleries leading to the bedding factory and warehouse behind. They now needed more factory accommodation so in 1880 they bought five houses next door to the shop.

In 1884 a new department for sitting-room furniture was started and given a separate catalogue. It contained a preponderance of 'occasional' drawing room furniture, Davenports', little tea tables, music stands, 'chiffoniers', ornamental wall brackets, over-mantels and so on. In the Health Exhibition of 1884, commonly known as the 'Healtheries', Heal & Son staged a completely furnished bedroom which was somewhat of a novelty in those days. This was followed by a series of six similarly fitted rooms on one of the upper floors of the shop, the earliest room sets.

From a retailing point of view, John Harris Junior with his energy and enterprise had brought Heals to the first rank of furniture shops in England. But it was his grandson, Ambrose Heal, who joined the company in 1893, who gave it a name for modern design. He introduced a markedly simplified type of design and sound, hand workmanship, unlike the machine-carved ornamentation commonly found in shops. This furniture was a rather crude attempt towards a simpler approach but from it there developed a style which became recognizable as Heal's. The first sign of it was when Ambrose Heal issued a catalogue of oak bedroom furniture made to his own design in 1898, which showed the influence of William Morris's arts and crafts movement.

Ambrose had trained in the workshop as a cabinet maker and had an understanding of materials. He was a successful pioneer who never lost touch with economic realities and his designs appealed to a new, responsible market, represented by young people who welcomed something different. The simple, well proportioned, structural details were neither disguised nor over emphasized; the colour and natural decorative quality of the wood was revealed. Stains, glittering polishes, carved and unnecessary decoration were rejected.

When he did use ornament it was with great subtlety, as in an oak wardrobe made for the Paris Exhibition of 1900, with inlays of ebony and pewter. All his furniture was essentially English in character. The furniture trade thought his designs were unsaleable and his own staff thought it looked like prison furniture. Ambrose Heal, like Terence Conran, was that rare combination: a designer with an adventurous imagination and an inspiration for shopkeeping. His work helped to change the whole conception of furnishing by getting away from the tyranny of 'period styles'. And his influence was evident in the catalogues too where his interest in typography and lettering showed in the choice of bold, well formed letters, with a black and white chequer board device which was a feature of Heal's advertising for over thirty years.

Ambrose retired in 1960 and his sons Anthony and Christopher took over. In the early seventies they brought in a managing director from outside with no experience or understanding of the furniture business and they began to try and beat other sorts of furniture retailers at their own game. They started importing, from Scandinavia and Italy, vastly expensive, vastly grand, vastly foreign furniture. Anthony's son Oliver worked his way through every department and took over as managing director in 1980, but he had neither the confidence nor the aggression to put things right. A few months after Conran took over, Oliver left, though his father stayed on for a year to 'keep the continuity'.

During the late seventies and early eighties, when Heal's had started to lose money, their standards had slipped. As far as products were concerned their policy was 'if it'll make money we'll have to sell it'. There was more and more merchandise with nothing to recommend it except mainstream acceptability. Each year sales never quite covered costs, nor did they maintain their reputation for good quality, simple, stylish goods, and the back up services became increasingly impoverished.

Geoff Davy, Habitat's buying director, was involved in the negotiations for Heal's from early on. 'The idea of buying Heal's was floated over dinner one evening in Paris. Then I found it was a bit more than just a dream: Terence had already had some talks with Heal's. In February there were more conversations with them and myself and Chris Turner our chief executive.' When Conran formally bought the business in February 1983, Geoff Davy became managing director. He came in two days a week from then until April. He joined the board straight away and he walked around the store, talked to people, found out how it worked. The cost structure was examined and the salary structure. The merchandise was changed, 'getting it back to standards it should never have moved from,' says Geoff Davy. 'If sales slip a bit we have budgeted for that, because we are not going to sell any old tat. Going right back to the bedding for instance, the epitome of what Heal's is all about. These beds are well made and cost a lot of money. Where else can you find craftsmen so pernickety that when the screws are in, all the heads have to run north and south?'

It was decided to move Habitat from the branch up the road to the Heal's building and also to put in a branch of Mothercare and of the new teenage retailing enterprise NOW. Heal's itself would be pared down and prepared to be a prototype for a chain of stores and trade from three floors of the same building. The rest of the building would house the group offices, the Habitat Mothercare design group, the photographic studios, advertising and catalogue production and the archive room. Before any of this could happen it was necessary to renovate and convert the whole building. 'Every square inch has had something done to improve it' says Davy. The bedding factory moved to Islington 'with a sensible layout where it can be efficient and in a part of town where most of the staff live. We have to be careful not to lose these people.

'When the new management took over, everybody knew Heals had been going downhill. There was a fear that the whole place would end up as a car park or that some ruthless retailer would come in and scrap all the traditions. They were very frightened that we would be ruthless. We gave all the directors offers and several chose not to take them. On that day probably we did look a real bunch of bloodthirsty beggars, because that day the management was decimated,' said Geoff Davy. 'But people who stayed, like the guy who runs the factories, were very optimistic. Young management felt as though the cellar roof had been taken away and they were seeing daylight for the first time: if it rained, or the sun shone through – well, it was all up to them. We had optimism from the suppliers and optimism in the shops. They had thought we would make 150 people redundant and we didn't make anybody redundant.'

Les Meldrum, the architect in charge, worked 'day and night', in the Habitat tradition, to get the building ready. He had been job architect for Arhends Burton and Koralek when the extension to the Wallingford building was added in 1980. With six people he began splitting up the Heal's building. 'The newer part of the building designed by Fitzroy Robinson is really a cheap copy of the original and has not been highly successful. If you walk past the front of the shop you will see that the older building has rather fine stone columns, whereas the newer ones are squared concrete. The fitments for the shop have oak edging, very expensive objects to produce, but in the long run they will reinforce the feeling of quality. The cast iron columns were exposed, the lantern roof lights upgraded and reglazed.' The columns are very elegant. The most controversial change was the removal of the curved glass from the front windows. 'I thought this was vandalism at first. But it was just a retail fashion really – and of course the curve wasn't there when the building was originally put up.' Heal's have two water colour paintings of the shop as it was, with plain glass windows. Heal's own workshops did a lot of the work. 'The really interesting thing about the skilled craftsmen is their attitude to a job. We were trying to get them to do fitments for us and it was not the normal architect/supplier relationship at all. They insisted on quality and they just walked away when you suggested making something cheaper. They'd say "Look, if you want a cheap job, just go elsewhere."

'Heals has been a very very difficult job and I've never been happier in my whole life. I worked sixty or seventy hours a week and I didn't get tired. I lost two stone and hadn't been working with Terence long enough to learn better ways, so I just told him what I thought. One good thing about Habitat is that they interfere so little.' Thus was planned, as Oliver Gregory put it, a renaissance. 'What we want to do is turn the store back into Heals' he said. 'There's a danger it may become crafty and precious but we want to have the quality and uniqueness that Heals had. We may even design a special range of furniture here. Heal's has not lost its reputation with the public. It has a name for reliability, quality, good taste, well made furniture, excellent beds. It has an aura of excellence round it.'

The purchase of Heal's took place very quickly after the Mothercare merger and the process of turning the store into the Habitat Mothercare's group headquarters, incorporating a Habitat store, a Mothercare and a Heal's was complete within a year. The plan for Heal's is to adapt the company so that its existing two outlets in Guildford and London can be expanded to about fourteen, using the thirty-eight-strong network of Habitats as the guide. Heal's' 20,000 lines of furniture were cut to something more like 4 500, of basically English, modern furniture of traditional good quality, including the splendid Heal's beds. Sadly, Conran thinks there is not the mass demand in Britain for the aesthetic approach to home furnishings you find, say, in Milan. 'We hope to get back a little of what Ambrose Heal had to offer, an Englishness of design. Thus it is felt the stores will be able to hold on to those customers who have furnished their first and second homes from Habitat, but are now moving into their forties, and are tending to look for something a bit more solid. I can see four Heal's stores in London and another eight in places like Bristol, Manchester and Edinburgh.'

12 Terence Orby Conran

PEOPLE who knew Conran as a young man never doubted he would be a success. 'There were about a dozen people, I suppose, who one felt were going to do something tremendous,' says Mary Quant, who is undoubtedly another of the great talents of that generation. 'Terence had an extraordinary presence. You had a feeling of insatiable energy and perseverance. Also a sardonic manner. Ken Tynan had such a personality too, and Anthony Armstrong Jones (now Lord Snowdon). Terence has a wonderful smile, which seems radiant and expresses a joy in life, a big appetite for food and women – highly attractive.'

So what is the secret of that success? Perhaps it is that Conran actually has no secrets but always declared his intentions and his views, and then had the confidence to try them out on the rest of the world. From the moment he entered art college his career has been based upon a strong commitment to his own ideas. He always appears to have known where he wanted to go, even though he changed direction more than once, and equally important, he has never attempted anything unless he could build it and make an impact. When he made furniture in his old work-shops, he was determinedly attempting to produce modern designs and get them into people's homes and offices. The Soup Kitchens filled a gaping hole in London's restaurant circuit and achieved what Conran had set out to do, providing delicious, good value and filling food in fresh, attractive surroundings.

In anything he has done he has wanted to shine and to influence as many people as possible. He certainly has a lust for power but never for power over individuals, power for its own sake, or power in the political sense. He has changed the way we live and that is the ultimate expression of his power.

John Stephenson has been a close colleague since the 1950s and he has a clear sense of Conran's motivation: 'What's driven him is power in the best sense, an ideal. The power hunger is fulfilled now by the sheer scope of the business. The ideal is Habitat and the design group, neither of which is ideal, of course, but both proceed with a commitment and vision.'

If Conran's strength comes from his deep and utter conviction in his own ideas and goals, and if his motivation comes from his need to make an impact and influence the world, he could still have failed miserably were it not for two other important aspects of his personality. The first is his extraordinary design sense and his ability to know, almost by instinct, what is going to be fashionable. He once said that 'the curse of the contemporary is gimmickness' and he has always steered clear of gimmicks. At a time when London led the world in areas of style, Habitat opened with a flourish and was immediately *the* place to shop for furniture and houseware. At the time, it could have been dismissed as a trendy boutique selling cheap and cheerful products for fashionable young things. Yet had it been that alone it would not have developed into a thriving chain which has become an established institution in Britain. Established it is, but staid it is not. Fashionable young things continue to pass through its bright doors alongside everyone else.

Conran may have brought us pine, paper lanterns and bold colours but he also stocked high tech furniture and fittings long before they became popular and he will continue to be one step ahead.

His appreciation for good design is strongly linked to his delight in things solid, functional, unpretentious and lasting. 'It's curious that it's impossible to find an ugly hand tool,' he remarked to Stephen Bayley when an exhibition of tools was being prepared at the Boilerhouse. With Habitat he was influenced by what he calls 'below stairs' furniture – the sort he imagines would have been found in servants halls in days gone by. Interior designer David Hicks once pointed out that he had made 'upstairs' desirable to the lower middle classes, while Conran has made 'below stairs' the last word in interior chic.

The other quality which has helped him achieve so much is his business acumen – he is a gifted entrepreneur. Dan Johnston joined the Design Council in 1953 and has known Conran and followed his development since those early days. He was head of pattern at the Design Council and remembers being quite appalled at Conran's way of working: 'We were looking for perfectionism but Terence was prepared to have the strangest merchandise in Habitat – odd items of furniture from Poland, for instance, almost peasantware. All those successful people in that period had this entrepreneurial spirit – getting on with things, somehow finding the money and pushing the product out. It sometimes appeared to be happening in a rather slapdash way. The same applies to Bernard Ashley. He and his wife, Laura Ashley, were desperately struggling away to make a living and not succeeding. When Terence was making his furniture, they were printing scarves and tea towels. Bernard came to the same conclusion as Terence, that there was no future in trying to work the retail trade; his only hope was to do his own retailing. Laura started to design dresses instead of tea towels and away they went; their first shop must have coincided very closely with the first Habitat. Yet if you walked around Bernard's factory in Wales, you'd never seen such an appalling mess. Everything thrown about all over the place, with no emphasis on standards.'

It is the entrepreneur in Conran that manages to sustain a very difficult balancing act with Habitat – weighing up the elements of design, quality, price and adequate profit margins. He may have appeared slapdash but his shop was, from the beginning, remarkably well judged and his goods were always regarded as value for money rather than as cheap and nasty.

Barney Goodman, chairman of Mothercare, has worked with Conran for only a short time. 'I've been number two to some very brilliant men. Joe Hyman was "well to do" to begin with and Selim Zilkha was always a rich man. Terence really had nothing. On the way he has learned to deal with bankers, to take advice – he has become a knowledgeable, in-depth man. I'm fascinated with his ideas and I have a lot of respect for him and for his close colleagues, John Stephenson and Ian Peacock. Habitat Mothercare has become a big group from something quite small and that has taken a lot of managing. It surprises me the number of things Terence is able to deal with at one time. He's got two great assets apart from design: he's highly intuitive and he retains and understands everything he reads – an enormous strength in a business like this which always has masses of reports. He's a completely self-made man with a huge fortune and he started from nothing. That's admirable really.'

He started without capital and pushed ahead on his own, driven partially by respect for what others were achieving. He was only twenty-five when he said: 'Everyday brings problems with personnel, or delivery dates, new tools or more space – or suddenly finding that someone else is doing something better than we do it. I just saw a student's design exhibition. To see all that magnificent work makes me feel old. That's what we have to keep up with.'

He did not find he had a natural affinity with business finance when he was running his own small business and he worried endlessly about money. He found his friend Alexander Plunkett-Green was far more relaxed as he handled his wife, Mary Quant's, first shop Bazaar. 'In Alexander's flat,' Conran says, 'there'd be a heap of writs inside the front door, absolutely piles of writs, but he had much more style. I'd pay mine at the thought of court proceedings. Alexander floated along in an upper class cloud of unconcern. I admired that.'

When he left Ryman, one of his first priorities was to seek top financial advice and to secure senior financial staff for Habitat. A colleague says, 'Terence is supreme, except for the nitty gritty of finance and he has chosen very expert professional people to cope with that for him. Ian Peacock, group finance director, gives consistently good advice. He's a nice man, pedantic to a degree, but that's what you need for an accountant.'

Conran's entrepreneurism and his energy are well-disciplined by colleagues such as Peacock to produce a hard-headed approach to business. It can sometimes appear to the public that Conran has suddenly had a flash of inspiration and rushed into a new line or project almost overnight. It is not so; every move he makes is carefully planned. He thought about opening a shop for many years before he actually decided to go ahead. He likes to formulate plans long in advance, getting the germ of an idea and letting it simmer. And testing it against his colleagues. The creation of the Basics range of furniture is an example. Tony Maynard had managed to clear a substantial backlog of stock at one point when the retail market was affected by a general malaise. Maynard had done a careful promotion and lowered prices. As ever, Conran created an advantage from what had been a difficult period for Habitat. Colleagues say that for about eighteen months following this, Conran repeatedly muttered: 'I'm sure there's something here.' The something was to establish a range of versatile, simple and inexpensive furniture to appeal specifically to young people in rented property or setting up home, and to promote it well and stress its good value.

The idea for 'mini shops', in which furniture is displayed to a limited extent and customers can discuss the range, colours and details with staff and order their purchases, was first discussed in 1976. Conran toyed with the concept for a few years before the first store was opened, in Lincoln, as an experiment. It can appear from his reactions sometimes that he has future plans which he is keeping guardedly to himself. He does stress the importance of thinking things through. Perhaps the one time he did rush into something was the merger with Ryman. He certainly learned a serious lesson as a result.

The decision to make Habitat a public company followed a long process of deliberation and preparation. The top management actually acted as if it were a public company for some time before it was finalized, in anticipation of the event. Morgan Grenfell, the merchant bank, were involved two years before the company was listed. Roger Selig, of Morgan Grenfell, was invited on to the board as a part time director. The change has opened up new horizons for Habitat but has created problems as well.

Ian Peacock is an old hand at coping with the speculations which can seriously affect the company. 'The city is like an old woman's tea shop. It thrives on rumours and counter rumours. It is interesting and frustrating and you always have to be on your guard. We get followed very closely by the brokers and analysts who are writing reports and circulars and trying to persuade their clients to buy particular stock.

They are always questioning, always wanting news. They know, and you know, that you have to restrict your information to the generalization and clarification of already published figures, but they try to catch you out so they have an edge over their rivals. But we have taken a firm line, we are always going to structure our contacts with the brokers. We'll give press conferences and see everybody at the same time, tell them all the same thing. We are still going to be followed by the serious ones and it is in our interest to drop the odd hint and to keep sweet certain key brokers and analysts who can say odd subtle things which can change a point of view which was wholly erroneous. Institutional investors come into this too and are kept well informed.'

In a general sense the City has become a customer as much as the public and those who need to know what is happening in the group are given regular briefing sessions by Conran and Ian Peacock.

It is seen as essential that the group should continue to expand. When Habitat was recreated as a company, in 1970–71, the annual turnover was £2.5 million. After the merger with Mothercare in 1981 the group's annual turnover was £250 million. By 1983 it was £380 million. Ian Peacock sees expansion as part of the motivation behind Habitat. 'One reason is that eventually individual stores reach saturation point and are unable to sell more merchandise. You can go no further with that particular store. It is essential to keep moving on and outward.' Conran believes expansion is important for the morale of the personnel within the company. 'People need challenges and are excited by them. If a company stays still and there are no new projects, although this may be satisfying for a period, very soon any ambitious people will want to do something new, strain themselves, expand their horizons, or they will leave. I'd hate to be involved in a business which was losing all the good people to other companies because of remaining stationary. One should always be aware of new ventures, provided one does not forget about the old ones. The company could steal businesses from less successful retailers but we are interested in a much wider expansion than that. We have a new store opening programme and already staff are complaining that they haven't enough stores to open. "Why haven't you got more sites lined up?" they say. People want their challenges and to do things better. And as the company grows, our wages grow too. Our staff are shareholders in the business and keen that it should succeed and grow for them as well.'

An article in *Design* magazine quoted a top member of management as having said in *The Times* that 'the company's philosophy was "making money"'. And the majority of people would assume that a man at the head of a dynamically expanding business would be motivated, at least to some extent, by an avaricious streak. 'Terence can't understand that the world might see him like that. He really has a vision that he is going to make people's lives better. He is driven by a social mission. One word crops up very often with him and that's "sad"; he feels sad when he sees people living in ugly surroundings. The people who deny his vision are the people who don't know him, the people who call him "Terry". He feels strongly about waste, can't stand that – in a metaphorical as well as a physical sense.' John Mawer remembers finding a crumpled piece of unused paper on his desk one day with a note from Conran saying, 'I found this in your waste paper basket. Why hasn't it been used?' People also remember that when, in the early sixties, the small company Conran then headed had its headquarters in Hanway Place, no one was allowed to use the lift (except John Mawer who has lost a leg) because it would waste electricity.

His close friend, art dealer Kasmin, feels Conran does not display enough extravagance: 'I cannot persuade him to put a tennis court in at Barton Place and I doubt if he'll ever have a Rolls Royce. For ten years now, I've had my shirts made to measure, but I wouldn't be surprised if he gets his at Marks and Spencers. Terence rents his video set, I bought mine. There's the difference. I live like a millionaire, he is one.' Stephen Bayley confirms this view of Conran as the rich man whose wealth is a sideline in his success. 'Terence has no rooted objection to making money, but it is fundamentally unimportant to him. What is important is to remove what he sees as clutter and improve people's environment.

Suburban, if he describes something as "suburban", that is the most devastating term Terence can exocet someone with, and, of course, the influence of France has been enormous – Elizabeth David and the explosion of the Mediterranean across Britain, Apicella's restaurants, travel. Terence is obsessed – Habitat is really his work of art.'

This high regard for him as a visionary who wants, as Kasmin puts it, 'everyone to have a nice salad bowl', is one that most cynics will not accept. Many people, including a vast number who do not know him, dislike Conran. Yet it is his Habitat which comes in for most of their criticisms, rather than the man himself. A repeated condemnation is that what is regarded as Conran's flair for predicting trends hides the fact that none of the design elements he promotes are original. John Stephenson, who is now, after a long association with Conran and his businesses, design and marketing director for the group, points out the obvious: that there is little in the world that is totally original. 'In both the home furnishing and fashion world, there is a constant dog-eats-dog situation. I think we do, certainly other people do, take part in this. When I first joined, I remember taking a mould of a very famous chair and I should have had my bottom smacked. We wouldn't do that now. You go around the world and see good ideas and you take from them what you need. Designers have always done that. It's not necessarily with malice or premeditation. You see something abroad, and months later it may become relevant to something you are working on. You may not even remember where the idea originated.'

Michael Wickham, one of Conran's oldest friends, was once interrupted in mid-conversation by a question from his eight-year-old daughter Polly, 'What is a plagiarist?' 'I am,' said Conran.

Another popular criticism of Habitat is that it is 'tatty'. In the early days the shops were rather special, rather 'U' and exclusive in the sense that there were very few of them. They do not quite have that reputation any longer. However, the furniture is better built today and more closely checked. Complaints are fewer than ten years ago, so quality control must have improved. Perhaps one reason for such negative responses to Habitat amongst some sections of society is that they are now twenty years older too, and have watched what was to them a small, exclusive store turn into a major national chain. Their standards, and buying power, have been increased as well. 'We'd hate to lose the twenty-nine-year-olds,' says Conran, 'and it would be nice to appeal to the forty-year-olds, and it would be relevant.' It is not only a question of age but of status and wealth too, and both the new Heal's project, a chain of upmarket stores, and the Conran Shop, more experimental and exclusive, provide for those who would rather not be seen buying in Habitat.

Conran, the rebellious, angry young man, has become an establishment figure to some extent and his presence is sought on governing bodies and boards both in the world of design and that of retailing. Conran was involved from the start on the SIAD, the Society of Industrial Artists and Designers. After a disagreement involving the ethics of advertising, he resigned, but was invited to return after the SIAD resolved that a little advertising was allowable and would not detract from the professionalism of a designer. Under the directorship of Sir Paul Reilly (later Lord Reilly), Conran was invited by the Design Council, to chair a panel of judges for the Design Council Awards. He has been on the board of the Royal College of Art, the V&A and many other design-oriented committees and conferences.

In March 1979, Conran became a director of J. Hepworth, men's outfitters. He influenced major changes in the company, including a shedding of the smaller, less profitable outlets, in order to concentrate on the larger branches. These were redesigned by Conran Associates. Hepworth's launched the Next chain of womenswear shops in February 1982, aiming at working women between twenty-four and thirty-five with well-made, classic but stylish co-ordinates. There were 130 Next shops open in Britain by the middle of 1983. Conran had become non-executive chairman of Hepworth in 1982 but he says, 'If I had known that I was going to take over Mothercare, I don't know that I would have taken it on.' He resigned from the board in May 1983.

Sir Terence Conran retains elements of the unkempt young man who always seemed slightly out of place in the sleek world of design and big business. 'When he went to have lunch with the Queen,' Ann Sayer, his secretary and minder, remembers, 'he shambled into the office with his shirt tails hanging out and asked if he could borrow a comb. In the end, you can forgive him anything.' Kasmin sees some ambiguity in his response to the Queen's accolade: 'I don't read the papers much at weekends, and I'd no idea he'd been knighted. I went to Barton Court for the celebratory dinner and peered into the bedroom where Terence was just coming out of the shower with a towel on. "What's all this knighthood nonsense," I said. "What do you mean, nonsense?" he said. "Mind you, I'd never have taken it except for Caroline. It means she gets ahead of everyone else in the queue at the village shop." Secretly, he's delighted.'

At times Conran can appear remote, even shy. One of his close colleagues describes him as 'curiously vulnerable for someone so successful and with a reputation for being so fierce. He has a phobia about ageing and age, and is horrified about being a year older each birthday. He's haunted by the idea of youth slipping away.' Michael Tyson was not impressed by Conran when they first met after Tyson had applied for a senior job. 'His dynamism just didn't come across. He is generally hopeless at staff interviewing. He can't understand people from a different background and finds it hard to get through to them at first. Added to this, I made an embarrassing blunder at my interview. I mentioned I knew Terence's wife was Shirley Conran of *The Observer*. He looked rather cross and said, "She's my ex-wife," whereupon his managing director John Stephenson leaned forward and said, "She's my wife now, actually." I thought, "Well. This is a bloody funny business, for a start." '

Kasmin's first encounter was at a dinner party thrown by Philip Pollock where, rather drunkenly, Kasmin spilled brandy over Conran. 'I was terribly embarrassed and rushed off to get a roll of lavatory paper and bandaged him up in it. He must have found this engaging because I was invited to dinner the next evening and I was a regular visitor at his home after that.'

Conran continues to be involved in the restaurant business with his Neal Street Restaurant, opened with Kasmin and Oliver Gregory in 1971. Food is more than a long-lasting interest for Conran, it is a passion. When Kasmin rented a chateau in the Dordogne for holidays, the Conrans would often join him in France. 'We liked to spend our time cooking. We had a big kitchen and would usually be cooking for fifteen to twenty people, including the kids. Terence suggested it would be fun to run a restaurant together so we decided to do it. We spent wonderful hours sitting under a vine in a little cafe overlooking the valley, writing notes on scraps of paper, working out how we should like our restaurant to be. We rapidly decided we were not going to have chicken on the menu. I wanted more cheese and I think I agreed to underwrite a cheese tray myself.'

The restaurant opened in September 1971 but Kasmin was not felt to be pulling his weight on the project. 'Terence always criticizes me for not being more involved. "God," he shouts, "there is that gifted, lazy,

Terence Conran's appreciation of food and all that goes with it is reflected in his Neal Street restaurant (*above*), opened in 1971. Caroline Conran, pictured with her husband in their kitchen at Barton Court (*previous page*), is a well-known food writer. Kitchen and dining areas were the hub of activity, also, in Conran's earlier homes on Regents Park Terrace (*top left*) and at Dalham in Suffolk (*top right*). Barton Court also has an extensive wine cellar (*opposite*).

Kitchens, cooking utensils and tableware have always been an important aspect of Habitat's merchandise. The Studio Kitchen (*above*) is a flexible and easily assembled range of units and cupboards made in British Colombian pine with white laminate work surfaces. Habitat's wooden plate rack, shelves and utensil rack complement the range.

Classic, French cooking pots were a feature of the first Habitat shop and the stores have always stocked a fine range of sturdy casseroles and serving dishes such as these earthenware pots (*top*). As eating habits change so Habitat provides a lead for the nation's cooks. Today Japanese Tempura sets can be bought and a delicious Eastern meal enjoyed from a new range of oriental tableware (*above*) in white-glazed porcelain, complete with chopsticks.

The Conran Shop has provided creative window displays on the Fulham Road (*above*) since it opened in 1973. It sells an upmarket range of furnishings and fabrics, quite distinct from Habitat merchandise.

The Habitat Housepack is sold through Habitat Contracts company. A home-shaped container can be despatched anywhere in the world to provide instant furnishing and accessories, such as this range (*below*), for a three-bedroomed house or apartment.

The Boilerhouse Project opened in the V&A Museum in 1981, funded by the Conran Foundation. The first exhibition (*above*), 'Art and Industry: A Century of Design in the Products You Use', made good use of the controversial interior designed by Conran Associates. An exhibition of hand tools (*below*) was held in early 1984.

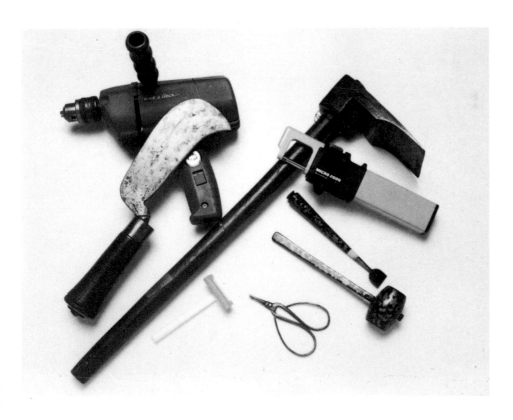

Conran with his family in 1983 (*from left to right*): Ned, Caroline, Sophie, Terence, Jasper, Sebastian and Tom.

Buying merchandise around the world is one of the most enjoyable aspects of Conran's work. He is seen here in India on a recent trip, choosing carpets with Jeremy Smith – the longest-serving member of Habitat's staff.

underdeveloped sod. Oliver and I were here on Sunday, Kasmin. What were you doing? We were on our hands and knees scrubbing, and we've arranged the flowers." He's got this puritanical streak – he thinks it's good for the soul.'

The private life of Conran the millionaire is not set against a background of old masters and high culture. 'He went through a phase of trying opera,' Kasmin says, 'but he went in at the deep end and got bored. He needs only three minutes to get a message and opera lasts three hours. I once tried to persuade him to buy a Ken Nolan to hang in his house. He got one of his designers to copy one. When I next went round to see him he pointed to it with great pride. "Look, I've got one now," he said.'

The Conran family, Terence and Caroline and their three children, Tom, Sophie and Ned, live at Barton Court, a large brick house set in parkland. A paved courtyard looks out over grassland and mature trees to a river beyond, where a group of fibreglass deer graze on the horizon. The house is fronted with a formal garden of espaliered apple trees and wild strawberries. The stable block, once the idyllic setting for part of the Habitat design group, is now used in that way again with two craftsmen from Parnham working there. Two ponies, a horse and four Manx sheep make up the livestock.

A professional gardener tends the large, walled kitchen garden next to the stables, and looks after the front garden and greenhouses. Conran takes a basket to pick salad for supper and admire his garden. 'Caroline and I planned it together,' he says; 'there was nothing at all growing when we took it over. We rebuilt everything, greenhouses, cold frames, though not the walls – the walls were why we bought the place. The whole place was completely and utterly derelict. This year there are butterflies galore. Asparagus is one of the real points of the kitchen garden. There's a really beautiful white clematis and there's garlic. We usually go out and plant the garlic in a sort of ceremonial way on Christmas Day. My mother always cooked and gardened, she was the person we got that from.' John Mawer helped clean up and repair the greenhouses and remembers, when cutting the lawn, allowing Conran's son Tom, then aged about nine, to have a go. He mowed under some trees where snowdrops were growing. 'Terence was furious and shouted, "Tom, Tom, can't you hear them screaming!"'

Conran hates clutter but the house is comfortable and relaxed. The kitchen has a fire in the grate and a television and a deep blue Aga stove.

Objects and prints are everywhere but to keep the atmosphere open and sparse, Conran says he clears out from time to time and puts things in the cellar. He works at home a great deal. 'I read through all my letters at the weekend and then on Monday morning I surprise my secretary by having all the replies ready for her.'

One of his staff had to see him at Barton Court on a Sunday. She found Conran with his son Ned who was 'behaving atrociously with bubblegum and Terence was romping around with him. We had horribly burned biscuits made by their daughter Sophie. Terence munched into them saying, "Slightly overdone, but delicious." That's a side of him people don't often see.'

Caroline Conran sees yet another side: 'I see the shattered shell. He totally exhausts himself. He's made the business with his own energy, force, determination of character. It's been a colossal strain. Now he's got a whole team of people and the world believes in him, it's slightly easier.'

Many people have described him as a workaholic with an abundance of adrenalin and fiery optimism. One colleague says, 'He's always coming in and saying things like, "This is the most wonderful day of my life – I've bought Harrods!" Then you'll find he hasn't at all. He's bought an old warehouse which belongs to Harrods, and he hasn't actually bought that. He has these hands that operate by themselves, with a lot of gesticulating and finger waving.'

Constantly active himself, he is demanding of his staff. As early as 1957, he was displaying this attitude to work. Wolf Mankowitz wrote of him then: 'The feeling that people around him are not doing things right plunges him into a state of anxiety which he can resolve only by doing the job himself – sometimes firing the incompetent who has thus wasted his time, but often not, because he hates to fire people. For although Conran has no particular close friends, he is not a cold character. It is simply that he has set himself a job without an end, to complete by a date which has not been specified. It leaves him very little time for inessentials, apart from sleeping.'

His close interest in everything that happens within the company can be a problem for the staff but he usually has a good reason for making a loud fuss. Christina Smith says: 'He will make an out-of-character, harsh statement if he thinks people are becoming too complacent. He has a meticulous eye for detail and would frequently pick up on some small point and bawl everybody out and you'd find it was terribly important and that he had in fact uncovered some big loophole in the system.'

Inevitably, many of the husbands and wives of his employees resent how hard he expects them to work. One member of staff says, 'Terence can be infuriating in his lack of respect for your private life. I find him ungenerous in this respect. He finds it difficult to praise people directly for what they are doing. He's embarrassed, doesn't know how to handle being nice to people and feels if he praises too much they'll rest on their laurels, whereas if he kicks them, he'll get the best. He knows exactly how to be awful. As far as the majority of us are concerned, nobody else's opinion matters. It's not because we're afraid of his temper, but because we respect his opinion.' He is well aware that his staff complain among themselves and feel they are being exploited at times, but he points out, 'When they go off to a greyer, less dynamic business, they find it's no fun without the pressure.' One of his first sales staff says: 'You didn't just give him eight hours of your day, you gave him twenty four. I admire him because he gave me a starry time. He taught us a lot and hurt us a lot.'

He can appear to cut people dead, stomping around the office or at parties, but this is sometimes as a result of his being blind in one eye. However, he has a formidable temper and is not afraid to use it. He comments: 'My rather poor temper makes life difficult for people around me. I can get myself into a poor humour rather quickly. I don't rule by fright or a reign of terror, but I suppose my intolerance can seem tyrannical.'

One of his staff feels that 'to work with him you have to ride his rages and pretend nothing's happened. He'll invite you to dinner afterwards and he never sulks. If you sulk you're out.' Another says: 'He's a bit of a bully, we all know that. But he has the capacity to give confidence to people too.' Anne Moorey, who worked for him as a designer in the early days, remembers: 'All of us had rows with him. There was a lot of shouting in those days, a lot of "bloodys". People were sworn at. He didn't tolerate fools gladly but he was never bitter that people didn't come up to his expectations. And the rows were never serious, more fruitful friction. If things had been smoother a lot of the things would never have happened that did.'

Another close colleague stresses that Conran never hesitates to state his opinion in the clearest terms: 'Even his worst enemy couldn't accuse him of being wishy washy. At board meetings he sometimes gets bullish

– lowers his head, sticks his jaw out over trivial things. Somebody may be a day late or marginally overspent and then he gets into a purple, table-thumping temper. But he's fundamentally a very kind man and he can't sustain it ... He's true to his star sign, Libra – vain, conceited, affable and never wishing to rock the boat. He has a reputation for belligerence, but few people ever get sacked by him. He is incredibly loyal and one of the least hypocritical people I've ever met.'

He shows how he feels on his face and has a piercing expression when dissatisfied. Maggie Heaney remembers 'a look on his face – when you saw it your heart sank. Once there was a photograph of him in *The Times* with that expression and I put it in my loo. My friends all laugh, but it really gets the bowels moving that look!' Ann Sayer, his secretary, has seen 'the look' perhaps more than anyone: 'His slightest change of expression tells you all you need to know,' she says. 'Terence is Terence to everybody, yet no one takes liberties. He doesn't care about money except for the security it gives to those who work for him – I don't grudge him any of it. Everyone looks to him for approval. If he doesn't attend the opening of a new shop, his absence remains like an open wound until he has been there. He might bluster and attack and criticize, but he is highly loyal to his staff. They have committed themselves to him and to something he loves and he will stick by them through thick and thin, even if he does lose his temper. What he can't bear is if they show signs of wanting to get away – even for a holiday. He himself is a workaholic, not as some people are because of desperate insecurity – he's highly secure. He just loves working. His idea of a holiday is to travel furiously. He can't bear to think of people relaxing for a second when he is not there. He can't take holidays really – he usually comes back early.'

Despite the tantrums and pressure which his staff have to confront, there is a general feeling that since Habitat is Conran's life and tremendously important to him, then it is inevitable that he should react strongly in any situation where the running of the business, be it day-to-day problems or major decisions, is being jeopardized. However, they also feel that his commitment to the company also creates a strong commitment to the staff and to their work. They find him remarkably human and approachable: 'We are all working for *him*, not some anonymous board. The closer you get the better he is, rather than the reverse. I have spent a lot of time in his company – not just meetings but on a one to one basis. I don't feel the least bit ill at ease, in fact quite relaxed. He has given me a load of opportunity. There is something about working with and for Habitat – it's as though it is everyone's family. And you get all the situations you get with families – emotional states, piques.'

A friend feels that he is 'a strange man in personal things, so difficult to understand. Gertrude Stein once said "When you get there, there's no there there". Finding the essential Terence is rather like that, he can talk about something with enormous conviction and then become so diffident.' Even his sister was surprised when she did realize how much they have in common; she describes a recent visit to India: 'We both sat on a pile of rugs. The salesman turned them over one by one and out of about six hundred, we chose exactly the same ones. Suddenly I found myself looking at someone I'd known all my life and thinking: "After all, I *do* know this person better than I'd realized and we really do have something particular in common." '

His power within the company and the force of his personality are undeniable, yet the petulant tycoon rarely outstrips the enthusiastic, brash and very human person behind that public image. Tony Maynard sums Conran up rather effectively: 'It is extraordinary to find someone at the head of a vast organization, as he is, being so accessible. Anyone and everyone can express an opinion and that's rare. When I worked elsewhere, it was an amazing occasion if you got a two-line memo from the managing director. It is hugely stimulating to work for a man like this.'

13 What Next?

A man with Terence Conran's energy would never be content to settle down into comfortable prosperity. The speed and energy with which he has shot ahead with new retailing schemes is startling. The merger with Mothercare, a chain of stores much larger than his own Habitat group, daunted him not at all and he quickly set about changing its image and within nine months improving its turnover.

The acquisition of Heal's has provided a prestigious London base for the company and a new retail adventure: the upmarket Heal's chain which will develop over the next period.

Still on the retailing front, and still with remarkable speed, he has introduced a chain of stores called NOW, offering smart, lively fashion in the form of separates, sporty casual clothes and accessories for teenage girls and boys. The first five test shops opened simultaneously on 8 October 1983 in Aylesbury, Cardiff, Hammersmith, Plymouth and Wolverhampton. The colours were vivid: blues, gold, jade, red and plum with more sophisticated black and white separates which could be highlighted with coloured accessories, and the NOW shops hoped to find their way into the teenage pocket with other merchandise which includes shoulder bags, watches, pens and pencils, alarm clocks, combs, ankle warmers, necklaces, key rings – in fact, all the things a young person needs which will not offend the parents. The intention is to wean children from Mothercare at the age of ten and lead them to Habitat in the life hereafter.

Having got NOW off the ground, on the same day in 1983 he turned his attention to women's fashions with the purchase of Richard Shops, a chain of rather unexciting womens wear shops. He managed not to have to buy their twin menswear business, John Collier, with all its problems – a clever coup. Richard Shops had a rather dreary image which would have to be radically altered. It lacked the loyal customers which made it necessary to make the Mothercare change so gentle. The Next shops with their smart interiors designed by Conran Associates and co-ordinated clothes for the well-dressed business woman – with flair but not too much money – have set a new retailing trend. A similar customer will be attracted by what is about to happen in Richard Shops.

Conran was on the board of Hepworth when Next was born.

Richard Shops will not precisely follow suit, of course, but will offer clothes that are easy to wear with that extra Conran style and fairly moderately priced. 'Richard Shops have everything to be done in terms of the design of the merchandise and of the shops themselves' said Conran shortly after the acquisition. 'When our design company designed the Next shops, it gave us the idea that we could do something similar for ourselves.'

Publishing is a new development for Conran. Both he and Stafford Cliff, creative director of Conran Associates, have had many ideas for books and Conran felt, as he had so often felt before, that if he was going to be involved in a business he could do it better for himself. The group already publish the Habitat and Mothercare catalogues, their own in-house quarterly newspaper and a Conran Associates newspaper, Habitat diaries, and a stylish Annual Accounts. Paul Hamlyn had been contemplating publishing books with Habitat and Mothercare for some time so they decided to do them together and form a publishing company. Hamlyn's tremendous publishing flair, best expressed through his highly successful Octopus list, and Habitat's practical and design skills, were pooled to create a company which ought to give the publishing world a shock and the reading public some excellent books. One of the first publications on the new list is a dictionary of design by Stephen Bayley and Terence Conran.

Conran's flair for property has moved him to take an option on a large part of the site at Butler's Wharf in London's dockland, giving him an opportunity to influence a wider environment than just the home. With Jacob Rothschild and Alastair McAlpine he is hoping to turn it into a residential, retail 'slice of life' area. The plans will be drawn up by Conran Roche, another new firm set up with Fred Roche who was at one time the planner, architect and general manager at Milton Keynes. The work will take three or four years and it is hoped to have space for an expanded Boilerhouse Project there.

The Boilerhouse exhibition space at the V&A Museum is, after all, only the first step in the grand plan for the Conran Foundation. In a rather larger area than the V&A can provide, it is hoped to house the most comprehensive collection of modern design in Britain, well documented and indexed so that students and young designers can come and study it. The V&A themselves already have a small collection of modern design. Not as large as it might be, due to lack of funds, it is in the main kept in the vaults below ground and therefore not on permanent display. Various sites have been mooted for the Boilerhouse collection, including the old Battersea Power Station, now abandoned and looking for a useful function, but Butler's Wharf seemed altogether a more likely spot and if the docklands are going to be revitalized the Boilerhouse will benefit from the new traffic and will itself help to bring people in.

There must be few people in this country who are not aware of some aspect of Conran's business, and few who do not have some item of Habitat or Mothercare merchandise in their houses. Habitat has enormous and obvious appeal, not just to the general public but the architectural and design world too, and has done for many years. It is puzzling that it seems to have failed to influence other retailers. By 1983, one or two stores were beginning tentatively to follow Habitat's suit, but they still did not seem to have grasped the need for identifying the market accurately or introducing a recognizable element of design. Some shops do, certainly, sell the latest items but the choice is haphazard and the eye lacks confidence. 'I wish there was a bit of the zip and entrepreneuralism in the furniture industry that there is in fashion,' says Conran. 'The biggest mistake retailers make is that they don't present furniture as a desirable commodity and make people want to refurnish their homes; they don't do anything to tempt and tantalize except hark on about price, price, price. Price is a very important part of the whole mix – Habitat only took off commercially when we realized that – but if you are not presenting a bit of a dream, a bit of excitement, people are hardly going to feel "We really must have a new living room".

'A retailer must know what customers' aspirations are – do they want furniture to last and last, or will they grow tired of it? Our job is to know that and offer what's appropriate; we've found that young people are excited by adventurous colour and style. They are more concerned with fashion and less with durability – though, in furniture and clothes, interest in quality is still growing. As retailers, we are not educators, it is not our responsibility to increase design awareness or put on design exhibitions. The consumer pays in the end whether it is for shopfitting, shoplifting or exhibitions of design. There would be more successful modern design if there was a greater demand from the buying public and that would happen with better consumer education. Schools and the media should be teaching people how to understand and choose products and, while retailers should take an interest, it should not become a crusading mission. Nevertheless, the retailer ought to be the dominant

144

factor in deciding what to sell, not the manufacturer, as in the old days. Retailers are in contact with the general public, they should be prepared to take responsibility for specifying and designing the products they want to sell, with manufacturers acting as suppliers. The ideal situation is when manufacturers employ designers in their own plants to work with retailers' designers – that's a new very positive development which we are experiencing. They need to work together to produce things to a specification that people are prepared to pay for. These days, price is important for a lot more people, including Habitat customers.'

Habitat Mothercare designers found that the manufacturers who had been working for Mothercare before the takeover were very enthusiastic about the changes they wanted to make, and not only in areas where they could see that the sales were going up. Manufacturers of clothes were surprisingly willing to fall in with the suggestions of the design group and the buyers. 'There used to be a time when any change was greeted as a disaster. Now it's "Oh, good, what can we do to help you on this?" Even producers who are deeply wedded to Marks & Spencer's ways are enthusiastic. That to me is the single most encouraging thing that has happened and it's very good for the future of this country.'

Conran's first intention is, of course, to expand the stores of his group of companies. Outside Britain, the United States is seen as the main growth area for both Mothercare, which is still losing money there, and Conran's, which began making a profit in 1983. So far Habitat's biggest foreign operation is in France, where it had twenty-four shops by the end of 1983, including the three out-of-town stores known as Grand H, a superstore venture likely to spread to other countries. There seems to be no reason why this rate of expansion should not continue. 'We are looking at areas of expansion all the time,' says Conran. 'Financial experts shake their heads and wonder where the breaking point will be,' wrote George Bickerstaffe in an article in *International Management* in November 1983, 'as Conran plunges into more complex problems of acquired growth.'

One limitation, of course, is likely to be the pressure on the management team within the group. The expansion in France and the takeover of Heal's stretched the management resources to the limit and the Mothercare operation, though doing well by the end of 1983, still requires a lot of commitment.

The responsibility of any large firm to the society it serves is not forgotten. The group has interested itself in various charitable projects, apart from the Boilerhouse Project, which is a personal gift of Conran's. Minor awards are made to various charities and Habitat supports the work of the British Trust for Conservation Volunteers, a Wallingford-based organization which promotes practical projects of rural and urban conservation for young people throughout Britain. Also, under the guidance of the World Wildlife Fund, Habitat is sponsoring the re-introduction of the Large Blue butterfly, which died out in this country in 1979. £9,200 of contributions has sponsored the transportation of the larvae from Europe to special sites in Britain during the summer of 1983. From a thousand larvae, it is hoped that one hundred and fifty adults will survive. If the test is a success, more larvae will be brought over in following years. In 1977 Mothercare founded the charitable Mothercare Unit of Paediatric Genetics at the Great Ormond Street Hospital and in 1983 the new group increased its support so that the research programme on detecting genetically transmitted diseases in babies during early stages of pregnancy can be developed further.

For 1984, Habitat Mothercare is aiming to raise at least £300,000 for the NSPCC through various schemes including a special design competition and other in-store promotions for the charity. Conran is a prominent member of NSPCC's Committee for Industry which has set itself a target of raising £12 million with many companies making efforts alongside Habitat Mothercare.

Conran forges ahead and the public, his customers, and the City, customers in a different sense, wait to see in which direction he will move next. One thing is certain, the entire team behind the Habitat Mothercare Group will be pursuing new areas for expansion, new areas of specialist retailing, new designs for their own ranges and for clients around the world. No one, even Conran himself, can predict where ideas and initiatives will lead. Habitat is twenty years old and if the next twenty years offer even a fraction of the excitement and impact it has created so far, then no one will be disappointed.

Index

147